THE FIFTH PHASE

AN INSIGHT-DRIVEN APPROACH TO BUSINESS TRANSFORMATION

DR MARK POWELL

T0312930

ADVANCED PRAISE

"Reading The Fifth Phase *is the literary equivalent of taking a double shot espresso before hang gliding off the shoulder of Mont Blanc. It is whip-smart, provocative and creatively potent. Armed with genuine insights from high profile and highly relevant case histories, the book makes sense of the accelerating mayhem of markets and the challenges and opportunities with the arrival of AI into the everyday, to reveal the real opportunities ahead. The brave really will inherit the world. This is where it starts..."*

Ed Will
Group Marketing and
Communications Director,
Brand Finance

"The Fifth Phase *explores, sensibly and pragmatically, how businesses can respond positively to the new explosion of data and machine intelligence. Mark takes us beyond the rhetoric of the day and the usual AI hype into genuinely useful approaches for leaders to adopt. He makes sense of vague concepts. He creates aspiration to create valuable new business models. He helps businesses stay ahead!"*

Anton Musgrave
CEO, Futureworld

"The Fifth Phase *is a fascinating read through the evolution of business transformation from a voice of direct experience. A no-nonsense perspective which cuts through the hype, providing in-depth insight and education on what works and, more importantly, what doesn't, when leading transformational change. A must read for anyone who to wants to stay ahead and achieve real business value from analytical technologies today and in the future."*

Maureen Wedderburn
*MMIC Supervisory Board Chair, CPI
(formerly, SVP Global Manufacturing
and Supply IT, GSK)*

"The Fifth Phase *takes us on a tour of our various attempts at business transformation over the last century or so: Scientific Management; Enterprise Resource Planning; and the various incarnations of process management such as Six Sigma and Lean Production. The book then tears an amusing strip off the Fourth Phase – the naïve belief that 'data is the new oil' and that accumulating huge amounts of data would somehow magically provide exciting business solutions. It didn't, and, as Powell says, many corporations ended up 'drowning in their own data lakes'. Powell's Fifth Phase of business transformation is data analytics powered by various forms of AI: 'insight-led and data enabled.' I profoundly agree that this new phase is a revolution in the making that has the power to allow us to reimagine how we do business. The revolution puts information at the heart of business strategy and demands that CIOs become more deeply involved in the development of core business strategies. Data analytics has the answer: CIOs around the world need to work closely with their C-suite colleagues to ensure we pose the questions that really do have the power to transform our businesses.*"

Roger Camrass
Research Director,
CIONET International

Published by
LID Publishing
An imprint of LID Business Media Ltd.
LABS House, 15-19 Bloomsbury Way,
London, WC1A 2TH, UK

info@lidpublishing.com
www.lidpublishing.com

A member of:

businesspublishersroundtable.com

Printed and bound in Great Britain by Halstan Ltd
ISBN: 978-1-911687-99-3
ISBN: 978-1-915951-00-7 (ebook)

Cover and page design: Caroline Li

THE FIFTH PHASE

AN INSIGHT-DRIVEN APPROACH TO BUSINESS TRANSFORMATION

DR MARK POWELL

MADRID | MEXICO CITY | LONDON
BUENOS AIRES | BOGOTA | SHANGHAI

CONTENTS

FOREWORD

Each year, corporations invest billions into Digital Transformation initiatives. The results, however, are sobering. At the macro level, economists cannot find a correlation between technology investments and productivity. At the micro level, a majority of business leaders describe their transformation efforts as failures.

How could this happen? At the core of this problem is a severe misunderstanding about what Digital Transformation is all about. Organizations need to embrace the fact that Digital Transformation is not about modernization. It's about value realization. As it turns out, modern technology has no intrinsic value and neither does data. Customers don't care about your technology stack or your brand new data fabric. All they care about is whether you provide incremental value to them.

Too many organizations are busy adopting the latest technology and get lost in the complexities of getting the job done. They lose sight of the purpose; the outcomes that their shiny new toys were supposed to achieve. They end up owning (and paying for) a sports car, while driving it at bicycle speed.

What's worse, they are driving that sports car without a GPS. We're living in a world of escalating complexity. We have reached the point at which reality is outpacing any strategy. Organizations need data-based direction to navigate the various dimensions of change that impact their businesses. Client expectations change with the pace of reality – companies need to do the same to remain competitive. To achieve this, organizations need the right sensors to capture signals of change that give them direction towards new sources of value. Backward-looking data analysis won't do the trick. A new approach is needed.

This is where Mark Powell's approach for an 'inside-led, data-enabled transformation' comes in. Adapting to the pace of change of modern technology, client expectations, and macro-economic conditions is hard. Mark knows, since he has spent years on the front lines, supporting countless businesses in their transformation initiatives. But Mark reminds us that we have a tool at our disposal that helps us navigate complexity better than ever before: Artificial intelligence is the key to unlocking the path towards a more adaptive enterprise.

Mark takes us on an exceptionally insightful and highly entertaining journey through the history of business transformation. He identifies the methodologies that have underpinned each phase of the quest towards more productive and customer-oriented business and highlights their drawbacks with immense clarity. These observations emphasize the importance of his recommendation for a better way forward.

I urge business leaders to pay close attention to Mark's point on focus. Stop collecting all the data under the sun. Instead, ask yourself which questions matter most for your business. Prioritize the data that can provide the answers. Interrogate that data to identify your path towards incremental value. In other words – focus on building your GPS.

Business leaders that take Mark's lessons to heart will not only benefit from tremendous focus on value in their transformation efforts. They will also be rewarded with substantially less waste and significantly lower risk during implementation. Hence, I cannot recommend this book highly enough.

As we embark into this new AI-empowered and highly complex world, it is essential to build adaptive organizations that remain focused on the value they create for clients, employees, and society. Scrap your long-term roadmaps and replace them with hypotheses of value. Test these hypotheses with the data that matters for your business and make data-led decisions on how to move forward. Let this book be your guide on your journey towards the fifth phase of business transformation.

Manuel Geitz
Principal Analyst
Digital Transformation,
Digital Strategy, and Innovation
Forrester Research
August 2023

INTRODUCTION

Recent world events have reminded us, if we needed reminding, that the unexpected happens and that the pace of technological developments is rapidly accelerating. Nobody expected a major land war to break out in Europe with the invasion of Ukraine by Russia in February 2022. Experts have been telling us for years that a new global pandemic would inevitably break out at some point in the future, but no one could have predicted that the breakout would happen in Wuhan City, China, in December 2019. Artificial intelligence (AI), which has been in development for last 70 years or so, is suddenly at the forefront of people's minds, probably in an alarming way because of the unexpected power of generative AI to create human-like text, audio, images and video.

It is becoming increasingly obvious that AI represents a technological breakthrough comparable to the development of the steam engine, electrical power, computing and the internet. We have become accustomed to the idea that many simple tasks previously carried out by human beings can be, and perhaps should be, replaced by a combination of robotics, computing power and the internet. We are just beginning to see that a whole new swath of knowledge-based and creative professions may be replaced by generative AI: translators; call centre operators; copywriters; lawyers; commercial artists; educators.

Generative AI is currently making most of the headlines, but it is not the whole of the AI story. The AI revolution will change lives as much as the arrival of steam power in the 18th century and computing power in the 20th century changed lives.

'Moore's Law', first formulated in 1965 by Gordon Moore, cofounder of Fairchild Semiconductors, suggested that the number of transistors in an integrated circuit would double roughly every two years. It became a shorthand for the idea that computing speed and complexity would also double at the same pace. People in tech are currently arguing about whether Moore's Law still holds. I think the more interesting debate might be about exactly how soon Moore's Law will become obsolescent. Quantum computing will operate at exponentially faster speeds than 'classical' computers. AI is already enabling us to solve problems that previously seemed insoluble using currently available computing power. Applying the power of quantum computing to machine learning has implications that are literally unimaginable. Moore's law is likely to look horribly outdated some time very soon.

AI is exciting and alarming in equal measure, but it offers the business world a remarkable opportunity. World Economic Forum founder Klaus Schwab envisaged a world where advances in a range of technologies such as AI, gene editing, robotics, nanotechnologies, advanced automation and the internet of things would combine to bring about a new transformation of industrial capitalism. This book will argue that AI itself is potentially the most transformative of these new technologies, because it has the power to supercharge the potential of each of the others. Its power to find new insights in volumes of data that are massively beyond the power of human comprehension will give us the opportunity to reimagine our futures. Schwab's imagined revolution is about to take place, and insight-led, data-enabled transformation, powered by various forms of AI, will be at its heart.

The central argument of this book is that the ongoing drive to make our businesses more efficient and effective has been through four main phases. Recognizably modern business began in the late 19th century, which saw the development of modern transportation networks, electrification, the telegraph and the telephone, mass manufacturing and modern business processes. The core driver of business transformation in this first phase of business transformation was Scientific Management: the application of observation, experimentation and the scientific method to the improvement of, first, manufacturing and, later, business processes in general.

The second phase coincided with the 'digital revolution', brought on by the development of the computer.

Enterprise Resource Planning was at the heart of this phase, which I have called 'Scientific Management with computers.' The core aim was still to create ever-greater levels of business efficiency, harnessing the new and increasingly affordable power of computers.

The third phase involved a combination of Total Quality Management, Lean Production and Six Sigma, all of which aimed to increase the quality of business outputs by reducing waste and error. These methodologies still have their adherents, and they have been demonstrably effective in a wide range of applications, but they are still variations on the drive for efficiency: taking an established manufacturing, design or business process and trying to perfect it by removing deviation and error.

The fourth phase – which we are still experiencing – has been at best the first step on a useful learning curve and at worst a waste of time and money. Driven by the mistaken belief that 'data is the new oil,' businesses have devoted a great deal of time and money to building and maintaining data warehouses and lakes in the belief that amassing enough data would somehow magically deliver new insights and lead to new business transformations. It did not.

I describe the fourth phase as being 'data up,' The fifth phase can be characterized as 'value down.' The fifth phase views businesses as a series of linked optimization opportunities and asks leaders to decide which key insights would allow them to radically reimagine their businesses in order to drive exceptional results. It views data analytics not from a technical perspective but as the enabler of this process of uncovering the insights that have the power to transform our businesses. Seen in this light, data and data analytics shift from being seen as a kind of 'business service' and become a central part of the essential issue of constantly reimagining our businesses so that they stay relevant and competitive in rapidly changing times.

Once business leaders have identified the potentially transformative insights, they can then ask data experts and strategists to explore the available data (which may or may not be currently stored in the organizations' own data warehouses and lakes), testing small amounts of data, relatively inexpensively, and using various aspects of AI (machine learning, large language models and the like) to see if they have the potential to deliver the required insight. Only then should they invest in acquiring large volumes of the right data. The fifth phase is still in its infancy, but a growing number of businesses are making use of the new methodology. Several examples are given in this book as case studies.

This fifth phase of business transformation is about reimagining our businesses and discovering currently unrealized business opportunities. It is radical, while the previous four phases have been essentially conservative. The problem with conservative, efficiency-driven approaches to business is that they assume the world will stay the same while we continue our efforts to streamline established business ideas and methodologies. But dramatic business success often comes from successful disruption. Constantly getting better at what we do now will not win the future; we have to be braver, more imaginative and more radical. We are still living though the impact of the recent revolutions caused by the arrival of the internet, GPS, mobile telephony and the mobile app. The disruptors who have successfully made use of these new technologies are now household names. AI will change the business world in equally radical ways, but almost certainly on a faster timescale.

There is a great deal of talk of these days about 'antifragility.' Nassim Taleb, celebrated author of *Fooled by Randomness* and *The Black Swan*, argues that the opposite of 'fragile' is not 'robust.' it is 'antifragile.' A robust structure might withstand more shocks than a more fragile structure, but it may still be destroyed by an unprecedented shock. Antifragile systems have the capacity to absorb such destructive shocks and respond in creative ways. Good examples (the only good examples I can think of, to be honest) are life on Earth and free market capitalism. Life on Earth is constantly stress tested: environmental conditions change; some species fail to adapt and die out; others flourish and become dominant. In free market capitalism, many ventures are launched and most fail; only the very best survive.

Business is currently being stress tested by post-pandemic and war-related supply chain issues and by climate change, inflation and labour shortages. The problem with the notion of antifragility is that it asks organizations to cope with these and future challenges by being as flexible as life on Earth or free market capitalism. It asks that we create immensely rich 'ecosystems'

– some of which will not be profitable right now – so that when radical change occurs, some aspect of the organization can rise and thrive, like mammals after the extinction of the dinosaurs.

That is not a viable business model.

The realistic and affordable alternative to true anti-fragility is creative agility: the ability of businesses to quickly adapt to changing conditions. AI and data analytics can help us make these rapid changes. We can interrogate the huge of amount of data now available about people's minute-by-minute behaviours to gain almost real-time insights into rapidly changing consumer wants and needs. We can model business scenarios of previously unmanageable complexity in search of the business models of the future. It is not inevitable that businesses must die and be replaced by disruptive competitors that are better adapted to the new realities; we have the power to transform our businesses in response to the changing world.

The fifth phase of business transformation is insight-led and data-enabled. The outcomes of this process have the power to change the world.

1

THE
SITUATION
CENTRE

In late 2021, the UK government gave the British media access for the first time to its new National Situation Centre in Whitehall, central London. The facility, nicknamed 'SitCen,' is situated close to the Cabinet Office Briefing Rooms (popularly referred to as COBRA), where the Civil Contingencies Committee, chaired by the Prime Minister, meets in times of national crisis, such as terrorist attacks, acts of war, natural disasters and other major incidents. The centre is protected against bomb blasts, physical assault and cyberattack. There are secure phone lines to other government departments and security headquarters, the military and emergency services, and to international governments.

The Situation Centre constantly monitors potential risks to national security. Its primary objective is to identify and prevent or mitigate them. If a full-scale crisis breaks out, the centre provides live-streaming information that can reduce reaction times dramatically: in the first two hours of a crisis, every minute by which response times are reduced is transformative.

I am a management consultant currently working in the field of data analytics. I have been working as a consultant in various fields for over 30 years. For me, the UK's National Situation Centre is a perfect model for the approach that business needs to take to the use of data and analytics: focusing on the most urgent issues — in the case of business, those with the potential to deliver the most value — and interrogating the most appropriate datasets with advanced analytics, to see if the data have the capacity to deliver the relevant insight.

I see the threats facing national governments as being similar to those facing today's businesses. They are sometimes literally the same threats, in the form of natural disasters, terrorist attacks, pandemics and outbreaks of war. But there is also the constant threat that our competitors will find some new way to disrupt our business; that we, as business leaders, will prove to have been insufficiently vigilant. And I see insight-led data analytics as a very big part of the solution.

* * *

One's first impression of the Situation Centre is of screens. Screen everywhere. Giant screens covering entire walls, broken up into a mosaic of smaller or larger screens, displaying constantly shifting images of graphically presented data, news feeds from around the world and video streams from selected remote cameras supplying live coverage of significant events. A glass-walled briefing room has sliding glass doors that can be closed off to create a private space. Two walls of the briefing room are filled with screens. In the main room outside the briefing room are two more walls of screens. The various internal spaces that can be created allow the simultaneous briefing of at least three groups of people. The main room is filled with banks of desks at which ranks of data analysts, each with their own double computer screens and laptops, are constantly at work. The facility operates 24/7, 365 days a year.

The Situation Centre was created to provide what former UK National Security Advisor Sir Stephen Lovegrove described as "data, analysis and insights to support situational awareness, horizon scanning and crisis response across the full range of national security risks — from civil emergencies to national security issues."[1] It pulled together, for the first time, data from a wide range of government sources, classified intelligence and open-source information, offering insights into 130 identified areas of risk. The facility aims to build as complete a picture as possible of various key aspects of national life by means of data, so the emerging impact of disasters and emergencies can be modelled almost instantaneously to guide the most effective response.

The COVID-19 pandemic gave the centre its first opportunity to deal with a major nationwide crisis. The disease arrived in the UK in January 2020, and the first national lockdown and ban on non essential travel was imposed in March of that year. A nationwide vaccination programme had begun in January 2021. By that winter, the potential impact of the weather on a successful vaccination rollout was a pressing concern.

I spoke to a manager involved in the programme, who wished to remain anonymous because of the sensitivity around all Situation Centre activities.

"One of the things we were asked from the cabinet was, there was a whole bunch of flooding risks coming in," the manager told me. "And the question was, what would be the implication of flooding to the rollout of the vaccine programme? Historically, it would have taken a long time to answer that question. We would have to talk to meteorology and ask them to give us an assessment on areas most prone to flooding.

Then we would need to speak to someone about where the vaccine centres are and start to think about which centres might be most affected. Then we would have to think about who was actually living in those areas, and whether they were high priority for vaccination. I'm afraid all of that was a relatively slow process. It wasn't that easy to pull the necessary data together; a lot of it only existed in different governmental departments.

"With the launch of SitCen, because we now had all the data set up, what we were able to do within literally two hours was to take the flooding risk, map it to the location map, then map on where the vaccine centres were located, then map on the demographics of who lives in the area, who was actually currently invited to get a vaccine. And we were able to see that, for example, 70% of the population in this particular area are quite elderly and probably won't have cars, and therefore you may need to exit them, you may need to physically go in and get these people to a vaccination centre or bring a vaccination to their homes. So by linking several available datasets, we could answer the key questions really quickly. That does involve a degree of machine learning, but that's not really the point. It's basically just information and analytics, but now we have live data streaming in real time. Pretty much as good as it gets. And that means we don't have to debate the numbers: we can throw the numbers on the screen within moments and say, 'That's the reality of the situation, so what do we think we should do?' More importantly, we can play with it. We can say — thinking about the flood/vaccination scenario — 'What happens if we add this filter, or apply this demographic, or increase the flood risk by 2%?' It's a compete transformation."

My contact went on to say something very important about applying data analytics to decision-making. "In the old days, ministers would have to make decisions based on relatively old data. I mean, sometimes literally published historic data, months old. With computerization, in some areas, several hours old at best; often much worse. And part of a minister's skillset would be in interpreting that data and saying, 'I think these data are telling us this, so the action we should take is that.' And, in the old days, if things were getting a little tense, you would get live updates being handed to ministers using fairly retro technology — like Post-it Notes. Bonkers, really. We've finally entered the 21st century. It's hugely exciting."

A lot of business still operates in what the SitCen manager refers to as 'the old days.' Business leaders make broad-brushstroke decisions based on relatively old information. And the decisions tend to be quite simplistic: do this, don't do that. Businesses in general are not set up to make decisions based on rapid flows of large amounts of data, because the data is not available in a meaningful way.

There was another aspect of the centre's work that I found interesting: the use of large language models to analyse public sentiment. There is a parallel to the business world. In the past, we were reliant on relatively old, relatively clunky consumer surveys and focus groups to give us an idea of what our customers were thinking and feeling, and what they might want from us as businesses. But the technology now exists to monitor consumer sentiment in real time. We will see a case study from The Estée Lauder Companies Inc. later in this book, using a variant of this technology to identify 'unknown customers.'

"Risks turning into crises don't normally happen on their own," my contact told me. "They're normally much more complex than that. They're sort of compound. Effectively, what you have is a set of planning assumptions in order to effectively test out your ability to respond, should one of these various things occur. And one of those assumptions is prolonged public outrage. If people are saying, 'Well, this isn't great, but we'll just knuckle down and get by,' you know? The famous British stiff upper lip and *make do and mend* attitude. If that is happening, we'll probably get by. People will weather the storm. But if there is prolonged public outrage — 'We're really not happy with this; this is unacceptable or unendurable' — then the current risk may become a crisis.

"With social media, of course, it very easy for a degree of public anger to whip up a storm. Public sentiment and anger is clearly one of those things that can pump up the outrage, and then you have the relatively new risk that bad actors that are deliberately trying to cause mischief are artificially pumping up the outrage."

The team looked for a way to ingest social media on various key topics and monitor it to distil real sentiments and other useful attributions, such as its geographical origin. This can help filter out deliberate misinformation. Not everyone has their Twitter geolocation tag turned on, so this might require analysing the content of messages and aggregating that to understand some of the context.

"It is equally important to keep in mind the 'normal' level of what might otherwise be seen as outrage," the manager said. "There are always keyboard warriors raising the temperature on social media, for whatever reason. You don't want to be raising an alert based on them. We need to monitor media every second of every day to understand what the level of real outrage is, above a broader tolerance. And that tolerance level needs to be dynamic. You'll have a massive spike in anger for a particular topic and then, over time, that's going to drop back down, but it might not drop back down to where the levels were before. The norm for that topic might now be a different level. So you need to understand that dynamic variability for threshold. This is where large language modelling is a complete game changer. It also doesn't only tell us about outrage. It serves as an early warning system if, for example, food shortages caused by supply chain failures are becoming a serious issue, or if there is likely to be a run on a bank."

Government ministers were delighted with the capabilities of the Situation Centre. Roger Hargreaves, Director of the Civil Contingencies Secretariat, which is responsible for emergency planning in the UK, told *The Daily Telegraph* in 2021 that "having a really powerful ability to handle and process data is at the heart of the effectiveness of modernized crisis response — and the Situation Centre is intended to be at the heart of that."[2] In a December 2021 *BBC News* article,

"Inside the government's secret data room," Stephen Barclay, then Minister for the Cabinet Office, told journalist Gordon Corera, "This is a massive step forward in our capability. The right decisions require the right data at the right speed."[3]

* * *

In this book, I will argue that the next phase of business transformation — the fifth phase — will be insight-led and data-enabled. Modern business has been through several phases in its ongoing drive to become leaner, fitter, better informed, more profitable. In the coming pages I am going to suggest that the first two phases were Scientific Management, which applied the scientific method to search for the most efficient way of carrying out an industrial process, and the growing computerization of this drive for efficiency via Material Resource Planning (MRP), Manufacturing Resource Planning (MRP II) and Enterprise Resource Planning (ERP).

With our enterprises all 'computered up,' we began to use increasingly sophisticated and largely statistical techniques in the search for quality and a dramatic reduction in defects. Six Sigma was perhaps the best example. Lean Manufacturing was the more experience-driven, less statistical sister of Six Sigma, and Lean Six Sigma was arguably the epitome of this third phase, which, interestingly, began to move beyond manufacturing and into service industries, such as finance and healthcare, and even into aspects of industrial design.

I see all of the first three phases as evolving in a straight line from Scientific Management — the application of science to improve the efficiency and effectiveness of business processes. The fourth phase of business transformation was driven by dramatic advances in relational databases, leading to the development of data warehouses and lakes. This went hand in hand with the belief that 'data is the new oil.' This was understandable, because the arrival of big data was opening up some exciting new possibilities. Unfortunately, in the 'dash for data' many businesses became obsessed with acquiring data for data's sake. Many built data lakes but never got to drink from them. Some nearly drowned in their own data lakes. The fourth phase has probably moved business forward, in terms of data handling and data awareness, but it has been an expensive learning curve. It is time to move quickly on from 'data up' to 'insight down', as I will argue in a later chapter.

Data represent simply another way of seeing the universe. The scientific method is based on the exploration of the universe as we find it and the testing of various hypotheses about how the universe might work. While we previously relied on our five senses, we now have sixth sense: data analysis, which allows us to explore the world via data.

In science, we never quite know what part of the universe may reveal the answer we are looking for. It's the same with data. We can never be sure which data have the capacity to give us the insight we want – so we should stop assembling all of the data we possibly can and then scratching our heads and wondering why it has not magically delivered useful answers. We need to decide what insight would be truly valuable to us, and then explore the data universe to see if it can deliver that insight.

Insight-led and data-enabled experimentation represents the fifth phase of business transformation. Enterprise Planning, Lean Six Sigma and the other process management methodologies have given us perhaps 80% of the business insight that could be available to us. The organizations that can acquire 90% insight into their business will be those that survive and thrive in the new business universe.

There is a huge opportunity for businesses to reimagine themselves with the help of data analytics, to think of ways in which they could be radically different; radically more effective; radically more profitable. Ever since the days of scientific management, business has sought greater efficiency through the elimination of waste and streamlining of processes. This is essential, unavoidable work, but it has two fundamental drawbacks. The first is that if it only delivers a temporary advantage, competitors quickly catch up. The second is that it applies only to known processes. Once we have a system in place, we can begin to refine and improve it. But the really significant breakthroughs in modern business have come not from process improvement but through dramatic new insights, often using new technologies to deliver disruptive new ways of giving customers and potential customers what they want before they are even aware that they want it.

As business leaders, our most important challenge is to think of the new insights that could change our organizations radically, rather than incrementally. Everything else is the equivalent of maintenance: keeping the existing machine running as smoothly as possible but failing to imagine new developments that might make the machine itself outmoded.

When we know which insights could have the most potential value, we can seek out the data with the potential to deliver those insights. And then we can use the remarkably powerful new tools at our disposal — AI, machine learning, large language models — to find the answers that may be hidden in the unimaginably vast amount of data that has quite recently become available to us.

This book will use several real-life case studies about organizations harnessing the power of insight-led, data-enabled business transformation. I hope you find them useful.

To begin, let's take a closer look at the early phases of business transformation.

2

THE FIRST PHASE: A SCIENTIFIC REVOLUTION

Ever since we have had 'businesses' in the modern sense, consultants and business leaders have looked for ways to make them more productive and more responsive to customers' current and future needs and desires.

This book will argue that there have been four main phases of different approaches to business transformation, and we are about to experience a fifth phase: a period of insight-led, data-enabled transformation with the potential to revolutionize the way we do business. Previous forms of business transformation have all offered, in effect, incremental gains: small but valuable improvements in efficiency and productivity. Insight-led, data-enabled transformation offers something far more significant: the chance to genuinely transform our businesses by harnessing the power of data and the astonishingly powerful new analytic tools we now have at our disposal. This creates the possibility that we might completely 'reimagine' our businesses through the insightful use of data analytics.

Recent faith in the ability of big data to deliver transformative results has been misplaced. Merely assembling large volumes of data and interrogating them with even the most sophisticated algorithms is highly unlikely to deliver useful results. In 2016, the research and consultancy group Gartner suggested that 60% of all big data projects fail. A Gartner analyst revised that outlook the following year, saying the figure was closer to 85%.[4]

* * *

In 2000, Chris Anderson, who was then the editor-in-chief of *Wired* magazine, wrote an article headlined, "The End of Theory: The data deluge makes the scientific method obsolete.' In 2007, Anderson was featured in *Time* magazine's annual list of Top 100 most influential people, which made me think twice before asserting that he was wrong. But I believe Anderson was wrong, and that the idea that big data would somehow magically replace the scientific method explains why the vast majority of big data projects have failed.

Anderson deployed some persuasive arguments. Google doesn't pretend to know anything about advertising, he said. It just knows that with enough data and clever analytics, it will be able to put the right advertisements in front of the right people. And it works! "[...] faced with massive data," wrote Anderson, "[the traditional] approach to science — hypothesize, model, test — is becoming obsolete." All scientific models are wrong, he argued. Newtonian physics was superseded by quantum mechanics, which also does not perfectly describe the real universe, so let's dispense with models altogether, because none of them is perfect. "Correlation is enough," said Anderson. "We can throw the numbers into the biggest computing clusters the world has ever seen and let statistical algorithms find patterns where science cannot." Talking about human behaviour, he made a seductive point: who cares *why* people do what they do? The data tell us what they actually do; who needs a model of human behaviour to give us the false comfort that we understand what underlies that behaviour?[5]

One problem with this approach is that it doesn't increase human knowledge. If we don't know why stuff happens, we can't do anything to stop it from happening in the future ... or make it happen again if it's a good thing. We have known for a long time that the so-called Mediterranean diet is linked to longer, healthier lives, for example. We noticed that people who lived near or in the Mediterranean region seemed to have longer, healthier lives. Then we began to carry out controlled observational studies to see if people who were given a diet rich in whole grains, vegetables, fruits, nuts and fish had did indeed have fewer heart attacks, strokes and other health issues — and the studies showed that they did. One study showed an additional reduction in cognitive decline and breast cancer.[6] Then, further research suggested that the key factor was the lower levels of oxidized low-density lipoprotein cholesterol (LDL, or 'bad' cholesterol) in the typical Mediterranean diet.

With that, we have learned something. We have a model of how things might work. We can try to reduce the amount of LDL in our diets. If Anderson was right, we would stop at the correlation stage. The data demonstrate a strong correlation between the Mediterranean diet and long life. So, eat a Mediterranean diet. Don't ask why; you don't need to know. Just trust the data.

There is another problem with Anderson's apparent blind faith in algorithms—as in "throw the numbers into the biggest computing clusters the world has ever seen and let statistical algorithms find patterns where science cannot." He talked, correctly, about the Petabyte Age. "Kilobytes were stored on floppy disks," he wrote in the *Wired* article. "Megabytes were stored on hard disks. Terabytes were stored in disk arrays. Petabytes are stored in the cloud." He talks about progressing from a folder analogy to a filing cabinet analogy to a library analogy – and says that when we get to petabytes, we have run out of useful analogies. A petabyte is 1,000 terabytes, or 1 million gigabytes. The growth of the internet and smartphones and the use of video means that the total amount of data in the world is now measured in zettabytes (1 trillion gigabytes). A trillion gigabytes is a lot of data. With that much data, an algorithm will find any number of patterns. The question is: do the patterns reflect any underlying reality? The work of science is to find a model that might explain a discernible pattern.

The belief that all data are good, and that more data are always better, has proved to be pernicious. It has led to a belief that building databases, data warehouses and data lakes is a good thing in itself. But data on its own has no value. Zero. We will look at exactly why big data projects have failed — and why they continue to fail — in a later chapter, but the simple answer is that business has taken a bottom-up, data-driven approach that quickly got bogged down in issues of governance, data quality and data management processes. This approach has led to many IT departments 'drowning in their own data lakes.' The data become unwieldy and inconsistent as they are pulled together from various sources. Governance becomes a nightmare. The data are never 'perfect,' so everyone is afraid to use them. The moment when the data will magically repay us with insight is always just around the corner.

We need to switch our attention to the big questions, the issues facing our businesses that have the capacity to unlock real value. Once we understand the kinds of insight that would lead to real value creation, we can focus the organization's energies on the search and identifying the data that have the potential to provide the answers that can lead to real transformation. Framing the problem in a way most likely to lead to a solution is a technique as old as human thought. Framing the problem in a way that enables us to interrogate unimaginable volumes of data, in the search for unexpected solutions, is as new as affordable massive computing power and access to zettabytes of data. The potential results are, quite literally, unimaginable, and they are hugely exciting.

* * *

Let's say for the sake of argument that 'modern business' began around the beginning of 19ᵗʰ century, with the advent of the Second Industrial Revolution, sometimes also referred to as the American Industrial Revolution or the Technological Revolution.

The First Industrial Revolution, which began in Great Britain in the mid- to late-1700s, saw the beginning of the move from manual labour and handcrafted goods to machine production, powered at that time by steam and water. It set the world on a path that would transform economies and individuals' living standards. Significant businesses sprang up in the First Industrial Revolution, especially in textiles and ceramics, iron production, transportation, agricultural machinery and chemicals, but the era is more famous for its entrepreneurial inventors — James Watt and the steam engine; Richard Trevithick and George Stephenson and the steam locomotive; John Kay and the flying shuttle; Michael Faraday and electromagnetism — than for the creation of new businesses that became household names.

In contrast, the Second Industrial Revolution, generally taken as the period between 1870 and the outbreak of World War I in 1914, was focused not only on invention and innovation (though there was plenty of both) but on dramatic improvements in productivity, driven by mass production, general business efficiencies, and the development of recognizably modern business management. Many of the great corporations that were created in this period have survived to become household names: the American Telephone & Telegraph Company (AT&T, founded in 1885, which later acquired the Bell Telephone Company, founded in 1877); The Coca-Cola Company (1886); General Electric Company (1892); Kellogg's (founded in 1900 as the Sanitas Food Company); The Ford Motor Company (1903); General Motors (1908). IBM effectively began life in 1911 when a group of businesses manufacturing time clocks, grocery store scales and punch-card tabulating devices — the business machines of that era — were brought together to form the snappily named Computer-Tabulating-Recording Company, which was renamed as International Business Machines in 1924, under the leadership of former traveling piano salesman Thomas J Watson Sr.

Henry Bessemer's development of an industrial process that enabled the mass production of low-cost steel in the mid-1800s drove the growth of many industries. The railways and maritime transport were modernizing. At the end of the 19th century, Rudolf Diesel received patents for an engine that converted a far higher proportion of heat energy into work. The first diesel-powered ships, trucks and locomotives would be launched early in the 20th century. Advances in electrical technologies were perhaps the most significant development, leading to the electrification of industry, and then households (although not until around the 1920s, and then only in cities). Communication had been revolutionized by the electrical telegraph in the 1840s and by the first submarine telegraph cables in the 1850s. At the end of the century, Guglielmo Marconi would invent a method of wireless telegraphy, the first use of the radio waves discovered by Heinrich Hertz in 1886, the year when Alexander Graham Bell was awarded a US patent for the electric telephone. The stage was set for a revolution that would bring these and other technological advances together to create the modern world.

If you accept my argument that modern business began with the Second Industrial Revolution, then we can put a precise date on the beginning of the first phase of business transformation. It began in 1911, with the publication of Frederick Winslow Taylor's *The Principles of Scientific Management*.

* * *

Taylor was born in 1856 in Philadelphia, Pennsylvania. His family were Quakers, congregational Protestants with a history of pacifism, teetotalism, active opposition to slavery and advocacy of social justice. Taylor's mother's ancestors — the Winslows — were among the pilgrims who sailed from England to Cape Cod, Massachusetts, in 1620 on board the Mayflower, seeking a break with the Church of England and freedom of worship.

He passed his entry examinations for Harvard University, where he had planned to study law, but chose instead to become an apprentice machinist for a Philadelphia pump manufacturing company, whose owners were friends of the family. After his apprenticeship, he worked in the machine shop at the Midvale Steel Works, becoming foreman and then chief engineer.

Taylor went on to serve as plant manager for a company running paper mills, and then worked as an engineering consultant. In 1898 he went to work for Bethlehem Steel, charged with improving capacity in the machine shop. He and a colleague discovered, through a series of experiments, that the use of steel alloyed with tungsten in metal-cutting tools greatly improved cutting times. The sale of the resulting patents to Bethlehem Steel made them both wealthy men. In 1906, Taylor presented a report on 'The Art of Cutting Metals' to the American Society of Mechanical Engineers, reflecting the results of more than 30,000 experiments conducted over his lifetime of manufacturing experience.

The scientific method — using controlled experiments to unearth general principles and discover the most effective way of carrying out a physical process — was at the heart of Taylor's approach. His work experience had created a fascination for what we would now call 'productivity,' the maximum output that can be expected from humans or from humans working with machines. In 1911 Taylor published a monograph titled *The Principles of Scientific Management*, in which he set out to discover the 'scientific' principles that underpinned even the most mundane workplace tasks.

The book opens with a reference to an address President Theodore Roosevelt gave to the Conference of Governors, held at the White House in 1908 to debate the proper use of national resources. Taylor quotes a sentence from the address: "The conservation of our national resources is only preliminary to the larger question of national efficiency," and comments that it is easy for us to recognize visible signs of waste in our use of physical resources, but less easy to recognize simple inefficiencies in other fields of endeavour.

"We can see our forests vanishing, our water-powers going to waste," wrote Taylor, in a surprisingly modern-sounding passage, "our soil being carried by floods into the sea; and the end of our coal and our iron is in sight. But our larger wastes of human effort, which go on every day through such of our acts as are blundering, ill-directed or inefficient, and which Mr Roosevelt refers to as a lack of 'national efficiency,' are less visible, less tangible, and are but vaguely appreciated. We can see and feel the waste of material things. Awkward, inefficient, or ill-directed movements of men, however, leave nothing visible or tangible behind them."[7]

Taylor came to devote his life to the eradication of these "awkward, inefficient or ill-directed movements of men" in the workplace. His speciality was to measure the amount of work done in a given period and to look for ways of producing the same amount in a shorter time. He refers to this exercise as a 'time study.' It was another engineer, Frank Gilbreth, who specialized in 'motion study,' looking for wasted effort — as in, for example, frequent journeys to a different part of the workplace to fetch a necessary tool. In a study of bricklayers, he cited the effort wasted in stooping to pick up a new brick and a trowel full of mortar from the floor, instead of having materials presented to the worker on a small scaffold at a convenient height. Taylor tends to talk about separate motion studies and time studies, and only occasionally refers in his text to a 'motion and time study', but his and Gilbreth's methods have of course come down to us through history as the 'time-and-motion study.'

Principles of Scientific Management was very much of its time. Taylor's experience of manual labour at Bethlehem Steel and elsewhere was with gangs of men who would carry out their allotted tasks: loading ingots of crude 'pig iron' onto a railroad car or shovelling various loose materials such as ore, ash and rice coal (small granules of long-burning anthracite) from one place to another. Regarding pig iron, Taylor established that the average worker's rate of loading was 12 ½ long tons (2,240 pounds, as opposed to the 'short ton' of 2,000 pounds) per day, but that a 'first-class iron handler' was capable of loading 47–48 long tons per day. Taylor sought out such men, offered them a higher rate of pay and established the ideal working rhythm, with regular pauses for rest, that would enable them to work consistently at this pace, over long periods of time, without fatigue or injury.

In the case of shovelling, Taylor established that the ideal weight for a shovel load of any material —the weight that would allow a first-class labourer to shovel an optimal amount per day — was 21 pounds. Because the materials were of different sizes and densities, this meant that the most efficient work would require specialised shovels of different sizes, each designed to carry 21 pounds of a particular material.

Taylor's work with skilled machinists in factories was considerably more sophisticated and required experimentation to discover things like the most effective machine speed and material feed, and the best cutting tool, to carry out various tasks in ways that were more efficient than the old 'rule of thumb' techniques that had evolved over time. This led Taylor to his conviction that working men and women, no matter how skilled, were not equipped (essentially, not sufficiently educated) to be able to calculate the most effective, scientific approach to their work. He concluded that this was a job that should be entrusted to managers, or what we would now call 'industrial engineers.'

These managers would analyse every task and produce written instructions for the 'one best way' in which a task could be performed. These instructions were then to be followed, to the letter, by every operator. Taylor believed that a large number of managers were needed in an industrial setting — perhaps as many managers as workers. There should be planning experts;

motion and time experts; a 'gang boss' to show workers how to set up machines and carry out their jobs with minimal wasted movement and time; a 'repair boss' to oversee maintenance and repair; a 'time clerk' to take care of reports, records and correct payments for work done; a 'route clerk' to supervise movement of parts throughout the factory. The managerialist culture of nearly all 20th-century organizations has its origins in Taylor's principles of scientific management.

To be fair to Taylor, he envisaged the relationship between manager and worker as a sensible division of labour, leading to a partnership of mutual benefit. Denying that his system would lead to workers becoming mere automatons following detailed instructions, Taylor wrote, "What really happens is that, with the aid of the science, which is invariably developed, and through the instructions from his teachers, each workman of a given intellectual capacity is enabled to do a much higher, more interesting, and finally more developing and more profitable kind of work than he was before able to do." It was axiomatic for Taylor — though not necessarily true in the real world — that those who worked in organizations using his principles would earn more, learn more and lead more satisfying lives. He had a laudable vision in which increased productivity benefits all parties. "Scientific management [...] has for its very foundation the firm conviction that the true interests of [employees and employers] are one and the same; that prosperity for the employer cannot exist through a long term of years unless it is accompanied by prosperity for the employee, and vice versa; and that it is possible to give the workman what he most wants — high wages — and the employer what he wants — a low labour cost — for his manufactures." Taylor declares that in a workplace that properly implements his scientific principles, "The most friendly relations [exist] between the management and the employees, which [renders] labour troubles of any kind or a strike impossible."[8]

Scientific management was not universally welcomed. Workers feared, understandably, that the discovery of potentially more productive working methods would lead to their being required to work harder for the same pay. Owners of factories where scientific management techniques were not being used were unhappy about Taylor's introduction of higher rates of pay in factories where his methods had been introduced, despite the fact that genuinely higher levels of productivity more than covered the increase in wages. Taylor, in fact was fired by Bethlehem Steel in 1901 after a series of disagreements over the implementation of his principles.[9]

In 2001, 90 years after the publication of *The Principles of Scientific Management*, the journal *Organizational Dynamics* rated Taylor's book No. 1 in its list of 'The 25 Most Influential Management Books of the 20th Century.'[10] The list's authors described the work as "The most influential book on management ever published" and went on to say, "Although Taylor remains the favourite bogeyman of the popular press, the fundamental principle of Taylor's philosophy — the rule of knowledge as opposed to tradition and personal opinion — is as valid today as it was in his time."

Part of what made Taylor a target for the press was his patronizing view of workers. At its worst, he assumed the existence of 'types' of humanity that were inescapably destined for certain kinds of employment. As he writes in *The Principles*:

> "Now one of the very first requirements for a man who is fit to handle pig iron as a regular occupation is that he shall be so stupid and so phlegmatic that he more nearly resembles in his mental make-up the ox than any other type. The man who is mentally alert and intelligent is for this very reason entirely unsuited to what would, for him, be the grinding monotony of work of this character. Therefore the workman who is best suited to handling pig iron is unable to understand the real science of doing this class of work. He is so stupid that the word 'percentage' has no meaning to him, and he must consequently be trained by a man more intelligent than himself into the habit of working in accordance with the laws of this science before he can be successful."[11]

This harsh view of people's predestined capabilities is at odds with Taylor's view of the potential for workers to learn and develop through exposure to the improved ways of working revealed by scientific management and tutoring gained from working 'shoulder-to-shoulder' with managers. Seen in its most favourable light, scientific management represents a form of valuable knowledge sharing, spreading the learning gained from scientific experimentation with various work processes via written instructions and person-to-person communication.

Seen in less favourable light, 'Taylorism' (generally used in a pejorative sense) established the persistent divide between 'workers' and 'management.' This stifles grassroots innovation by assuming that any attempt by workers to introduce innovations to the work process should be resisted, as this would represent backsliding towards the old 'rule of thumb' ways of working and away from the genuinely 'scientific' determinations of highly educated industrial engineers. The establishment of the 'one best way' of Taylorism is an additional element of built-in conservatism. If this is the time-honoured one best way, why change? Taylor's insistence on the selection of the most appropriate workers for each job — the right 'type' for the job — also prefigures both the positive and negative aspects of modern HR selection procedures.

That said, scientific management became a movement of real transformational power that transcended Taylor himself. The key notion of applying science and rationality to manufacturing and other work processes is at the heart of all attempts to make business more efficient and more productive. The assembly line revolutionized many aspects of production in ways that Taylor could not have foreseen, but the core principles of scientific management lie at the heart of standardized and automated processes designed to set the ideal pace of work and eliminate wasteful and unproductive movement of people and parts. There is more than an echo of Taylorism in the ongoing efforts to improve all business processes, and even in the three 'wastes' of the Toyota Production System (TPS): *muda* (nonvalue-adding); *mura* (nonuniformity); and *muri* (overburden-ing). As Jeffrey K. Liker, author of *The Toyota Way*, puts it, "Toyota turned scientific management on its head, giving the stopwatch to work groups who were responsible for designing and continuously improving their work."[12] This did indeed turn Taylor's recommended workplace hierarchy 'on its head' and empowered workers to make their own innovations in a process of continual learning and improvement.

3

THE SECOND PHASE: TAYLORISM WITH COMPUTERS

The wave of business transformation that began around 1911 with the publication of Taylor's book lasted, in effect, until the computer age began with the commercial availability of mainframe computers in the 1950s.

The first half of the 20th century was a period of remarkable change, with emerging technologies creating new consumer demands that were quickly supplied by new businesses. The list of significant new business areas driven by technological innovation in this era is astonishing: the growth of railroads; the birth of the automobile and aviation industries; telephony; cinema, broadcast radio and television; shellac and then vinyl audio recordings ('records'); the transistor radio. The move from craft workshops manufacturing individual items to assembly lines producing completed goods within minutes, or even seconds, had begun. By late 1913, Henry Ford's moving assembly line was producing a complete Model T Ford every 93 minutes. In 1972, workers at the General Motors' (GM) Lordstown, Ohio, plant that produced the Chevrolet Vega went on strike when the assembly line rate of production reached 100 cars *per hour*, meaning that workers had around 40 seconds to complete each task. "This is the fastest line in the world," a local union official told *The New York Times* during the dispute. "A guy has about 40 seconds to do his job. [...] You add one more thing and it can kill you. The guy can't get the stuff done on time and a car goes by. The company then blames us for sabotage and shoddy work."[13]

In time, autoworkers grew used to this pace of work. Writing in *The Toyota Way*, author JK Liker recalls getting hands-on experience on a Toyota assembly line at the New United Motor Manufacturing plant in Fremont, California, which was jointly owned by GM and Toyota. He was given a task that was allocated 44.7 seconds of 'work and walk time.' The assembly line at that time was running at a 'takt' time — the amount of time allowed to manufacture each finished item — of 57 seconds per job - so giving him a task that required 'only' 44.7 seconds meant he would have plenty of time to get the job done, despite his inexperience. Liker noted that the 'standardized work chart' posted at his workstation detailed 28 different steps that would lead to the perfect execution of his task, including the number of paces necessary to move away from the assembly line and back again to get materials and tools.[14]

Throughout this era, work processes and methods of production were constantly improved, refined and updated to take account of newly developing technologies (such as the transistor), but the general principles of scientific management still underpinned every effort to improve business performance. The first half of the 20th century remained firmly within the first phase of business transformation. This changed significantly with the arrival of the first commercial computer in the mid-20th century, heralded by the delivery of UNIVAC (the 'Universal Automatic Computer,' designed by J Presper Eckert and John Mauchly) to the US Census Bureau in March 1951.[15]

The demands of mass production drove manufacturers to systematize production scheduling to meet demand for finished goods as efficiently as possible, while optimizing inventories and the flow of work through a factory. The moving assembly line had created its own inexorable momentum, requiring that all the items needed to keep the line in motion were constantly available. The lack of a single component or the failure of any subassembly process would bring the line to a halt.

In practice, of course, only the simplest manufacturing process requires the constant production of a single finished item with one set of components. Products are manufactured to varying specifications; demand goes up and down; new models are introduced; it's lumpy. An obvious solution was to manufacture components in batches, so there would always be a ready supply to feed into the assembly process. No supplies of part Y, needed to manufacture component X, might be needed for several weeks, and then 10,000 Ys are required by next Tuesday. Holding large amounts of any item in inventory is expensive, and there is the risk that components will become outmoded before they're required, especially in fast-moving fields such as electronics. There is also the risk that component X turns out to be faulty when it is installed in the product being assembled, in which case large inventories of faulty Xs are a disaster. There is also the possibility that it is difficult to turn out another subassembly, item Z, fast enough to supply the assembly of the finished item, in which case production of Zs has become a potential bottleneck. These inherent issues led to the rise of 'lean' or 'just in time' manufacturing, which we will look at in the next section. They also gave rise to a great deal of focus on the business of planning and scheduling the production process to try to avoid these pitfalls.

Throughout the early part of the century, mechanical calculators and slide rules had been used to crunch the numbers required to determine the Economic Order Quantity (EOQ). This formula — intended to reflect the ideal order size, allowing a producer to meet demand without overspending — was devised in 1913 by Ford Whitman Harris, an engineer who had worked for the Westinghouse Electric and Manufacturing Company. Both mechanical calculators and slide rules are, of course, now museum pieces, although some old-school engineers and scientists still prefer to use a slide rule for quick calculations, rather than stabbing the buttons of an electronic calculator. But by the 1940s, the computer had arrived.

IBM quickly became the leading supplier of vacuum tube computers, though UNIVAC remained a player, along with Burroughs, Control Data, General Electric (GE), Honeywell and RCA. One industry commentator described the market as 'Snow White [IBM] and the Seven Dwarfs.'[16] In the 1960s, the JI Case Company, a manufacturer of tractors and construction machinery, teamed up with IBM to develop a system of Material Requirements Planning (MRP). The system's software ran on an IBM mainframe, using the only memory medium available at the time: magnetic tape.

Details of inventories would be kept on one set of tape, and weekly transactions on another. At the end of the week, 'passing the tapes' would create a new master tape that would give a picture of the current situation. According to F Robert Jacobs and FC Wilson Jr, writing in the *Journal of Operations Management* in 2007, order quantities were still calculated using slide rules and entered into the system, because the computers of the day were not able to calculate the square roots demanded by the formula established for calculating EOQs.

As Jacobs and Wilson note in their article, initial MRP solutions "were big, clumsy and expensive." Throughout the 1970s, advances in computing — notably, improvements in random access memory (RAM) and the development of new and more sophisticated software — enabled the integration of more and more business functions. In the late '70s, IBM introduced a suite of applications called Manufacturing, Accounting, and Production Information and Control Systems (MAPICS), designed to run on the new IBM System/34, a midrange computer that was far smaller and more affordable than the old mainframes. IBM's MAPICS software brought together every aspect of a manufacturing business, from inventory management and production control to invoicing, accounts payable, payroll and sales analysis.[17] The increased scope of the new software meant that the old term MRP (Material Requirements Planning) was no longer adequate to describe its new functionality. The term MRP II was used for a time, but by the 1980s MRP II was being generally translated as Manufacturing *Resource* Planning, to better describe its wider scope.

A raft of new software companies had sprung up in the 1970s, offering what we would now call enterprise solutions, including Systemanalyse und Programmentwicklung (SAP) in Germany, J.D. Edwards in the US and The Baan Corporation in the Netherlands. Oracle Corporation, founded in 1977 as Software Development Laboratories, and later called Relational Software Inc, offered the first Structured Query Language (SQL) relational database management system. It was written in the general-purpose, portable C programming language, allowing the creation of software that would run on computers from various manufacturers other than IBM, such as Honeywell, Hewlett-Packard (HP) and Digital Equipment Corporation (DEC). The move away from reliance by organizations on a single computer or minicomputer came with the development of the microcomputer and client-server architecture that allowed the computing load to be distributed across numbers of small computers. The software company PeopleSoft, launched in California in 1987, offered a client-server version of an existing mainframe Human Resource Management System (HRMS). The creation of such computerized HR systems was a big step towards integrating all key organizational functions into ERP, allowing the automation of all a company's core functions.

In the 1990s, the Gartner Group coined the term Enterprise Resource Planning (ERP) to describe this integration of all key functions — not only manufacturing, supply chain management, procurement and basic accounting, but also any business functions

necessary to the day-to-day running of an organization.[18] By the middle of the decade, ERP functionality had extended into 'front office' realms such as
sales, marketing and e-commerce, and into what was
described as 'the entire value chain of the enterprise.'[19]

The arrival of the internet and the subsequent
development of cloud computing completed the modern picture. ERP would not only integrate internal
systems, it would also connect organizations to the
outside world, allowing them to publish details of
requirements that could potentially be fulfilled by
previously unknown suppliers, encouraging increased
efficiency and innovation. Large organizations began
to insist that their smaller suppliers run the same ERP
software as them, encouraging a period of consolida-
tion in the ERP software market and creating a barrier
to entry for some smaller suppliers.

Although both MRP and ERP are most easily
described in relation to manufacturing processes,
their application soon spread into traditional 'service'
sectors: health, finance, education, telecommunica-
tions, retail and others.

One of the downsides of ERP is that it forced businesses to operate in a way that mirrored the standard
functionality of the software, leading to significant
business process re-engineering. Various surveys have
suggested that businesses spent between three and
seven times more money implementing ERP software than was spent on the original software license,
with substantial costs associated with staff training and management time.[20] Attempts to customize

functionality could create major issues with future software upgrades, creating a 'software straightjacket.'

One significant consequence of the growth of ERP systems, from an analytics perspective, was the corresponding growth in databases of corporate information offering a relatively complete picture of how those businesses operated. SAP's ERP software, for example, offered a data warehouse solution called SAP Business Warehouse (SAP BW), giving businesses the opportunity to interrogate data across the organization and review how they were performing both internally and externally. This was limited to descriptive or 'dashboard' analysis of the data, rather than any more sophisticated data science, but it did give business leaders something close to real-time data on how their companies were operating. It also meant that business was getting used to the idea that a set of data could almost fully describe their processes and operations, which could be interrogated to suggest new ideas about how to better run things.

This was the beginning, in my opinion, of the seductive but false idea that if only we had more data — data about our own business, but also about customers and markets and competitors and, well, *everything* — then we could use that data to run our companies better. It's not an entirely false idea, but it led to an obsession with data for data's sake, and the search for the perfect dashboard to present and analyse that data in understandable ways.

Dashboards give us a false sense of control and, more importantly, the illusion of insight. In reality, they can only ever give us increasingly sophisticated rear-view mirrors. They tell us how businesses are performing and how they are being run, in the technical sense, but they don't in themselves give us real insight that will allow us to radically improve our businesses. They don't encourage us to reimagine our business or to think about which entirely new insight would have the potential to transform our operating model, as opposed to enabling marginal improvements. The ERP revolution was a significant phase in the development of business, embracing the computing revolution and marking the beginning of the data revolution, as companies began to acquire meaningful amounts of data about their businesses, their consumers, their competitors and market trends. But in every other sense, ERP was simply a logical extension of Taylor's scientific management: using observation and experimentation to discover the most efficient way to carry out business processes, but with the help of computers.

THE THIRD PHASE: PROCESS MANAGEMENT

The third phase of business transformation was all about process management, as represented by various 'movements.' As we have noted, these included Lean Manufacturing, Total Quality Management, Six Sigma and the more recent Lean Six Sigma. The focus, as ever, was on our old friend 'efficiency,' but with a special emphasis on quality and the removal of defects. The logic, again, is simple and unassailable. A defect in any area of a complex operation can have knock-on effects that ripple through a whole business, creating faulty final products and services that will have to be discarded or, if unwittingly sold, creating unhappy customers, warranty claims and damage to the brand.

Six Sigma was conceived in 1986 by Motorola engineer Bill Smith. The name originates from a statistical term, *sigma*, that denotes the standard deviation in a sample set. A process that is running at 'six sigma quality' produces fewer than 3.4 defects per million. Motorola's original concept was clearly focused on manufacturing, and it reflected the telecom company's urgent need to compete with the extremely high-quality electronic goods being manufactured by Japan. It's a little surprising that this quintessentially statistical technique developed into such a mainstream management tool. That has a lot to do with GE CEO Jack Welch, the darling of Wall Street, who embraced Six Sigma with his usual messianic zeal in 1995. He announced that Six Sigma was going to be the biggest initiative ever launched at GE, and that he was going to make its implementation his primary objective for the next five years. GE stock rose sharply, even before there were any tangible results of the programme to announce. Welch was already a superstar CEO, credited with driving GE's market value to ever-greater heights. If he said that Six Sigma was going to help make GE more valuable, Wall Street was prepared to believe it.

Welch invested heavily in training, putting large numbers of staff through a 100-hour course and insisting that every employee take part in a certified Six Sigma project by 1998. He brought in mentors to train selected staff up to the famous 'Six Sigma Black Belt' standard, and said that anyone hoping for a promotion should have at least the more junior 'Green Belt' certificate.[21] By the year 2000, Welch announced that GE had achieved what *Forbes* described as "more than $2 billion in benefits" from improved product quality.[22] Corporate America sat up and took notice.

Despite its highly technical statistical models, Six Sigma quickly evolved at Motorola into a more obviously recognizable general management tool. Tom McCarty, who was Director for Six Sigma at Motorola, wrote in *EuropeanCEO* in 2004 that the company "has learned Six Sigma goes far beyond counting defects in a process or product. The next-generation Six Sigma is an overarching high-performance system that executes business strategy."

McCarty outlined the now-familiar roadmap for Six Sigma: Define, Measure, Analyse, Improve and Control (DMAIC).[23] The first step — Define, the selection of what business area needs to be improved — is arguably the key element of the process. By 2001, it had been added by GE and others to the initial MAIC process: Measure, Analyse, Improve, Control.[24]

Any business that devotes a lot of senior management time and effort to 'Defining' the key areas in its business that would most benefit from improvement is potentially already on the road to success. 'Measuring' the current state of affairs and 'Analysing' the root causes of business problems are pretty obvious steps. The next stage of DMAIC in Six Sigma terms, 'Improvement', is more significant than it sounds. It involves what are hopefully the best brains in the business applying themselves to the search for a solution. Having found a possible solution, the team 'Controls' the new process by monitoring it to ensure that it is delivering long-term benefits.

Writing in the *Journal of Operations of Management* in 2008, in an article titled "Six Sigma: Definition and underlying theory," Roger Schroeder and others set out to provide "a conceptual definition and identify an underlying theory" for the young but relatively under-researched field. They undertook research at a large ("multi billions of dollars in revenue") manufacturing company that had been implementing Six Sigma for three years. The article noted that the company had 350 Black Belt Six Sigma specialists out of its 10,000 full-time employees — 3.5 % of its workforce – and that these specialists did nothing but work on selected projects, reporting to a project 'Champion,' a member of senior management trained in Six Sigma basics.

Senior management was also involved in filtering out proposed projects deemed not to have "financial or strategic importance." The article described how the implementation of Six Sigma in this organization deliberately created "a hierarchical structure where leaders

(Champions) initiate, support and review improvement projects; Black Belts then serve as project leaders who mentor Green Belts in problem-solving efforts."

Although Six Sigma quickly developed beyond its original, mechanistic aim to reduce defects to less than 3.4 per million, Six Sigma projects were still driven by precise metrics, creating challenging goals that could drive results. Six Sigma was also very financially driven, with a focus on delivering measurable financial results. Schroeder and his colleagues identified the likely real key to Six Sigma's success. They noted that it allowed organizations to switch between structural approaches, acting "more *organically* in coming up with new improvement ideas and more *mechanistically* when implementing them." This, they said, allows them to deal with "the conflicting demands of exploration and control." To put it another way, Six Sigma demanded the use of business creativity before it imposed a process of measurement and control. The approach trained significant numbers of employees to focus on key business problems and committed senior executives to selecting the most significant projects to explore — those that were most financially or strategically significant. It demanded that senior executives and dedicated project managers (Black Belts) stay focused on one project until results were delivered. It set precisely defined goals to show what success would look like.

Six Sigma was generally seen as an offshoot of the wider-ranging Total Quality Management (TQM) approach. Motorola's McCarty defined what he saw as the key differences in his 2004 article. TQM was the province of self-directed teams; Six Sigma had executive ownership. TQM was focused on product quality; Six Sigma was about executing business strategy. TQM generally operated in single business functions; Six Sigma was applied across the whole enterprise. And while TQM was quality oriented, Six Sigma was business oriented, focused on verifiable returns on investment.

GE implemented Six Sigma projects at its financial services business, GE Capital, demonstrating the methodology's potential to transform any business process, not manufacturing alone. The Bank of America followed suit, and announced billions of dollars in savings. Six Sigma was taken up in the late 1990s and early 2000s by organizations such as Dupont, Dow Chemical, 3M, Ford, American Express, Samsung and the US military.

Honeywell, and later GE, applied it to the design process, where there had been no existing process to refine and improve. Design for Six Sigma (DFSS) was based on a process of Define, Measure, Analyse, Design, Verify.[25] Six Sigma had come a long way from Bill Smith's vision of a statistically-based methodology that would eliminate defects from a manufacturing process.

An executive from the manufacturing company investigated by Schroeder and his colleagues described the process very powerfully: "For us, you take from among your best people, give them four weeks of problem-solving discipline skills, you tie them to one of your most leveraged problems, that if you fix this it generates a lot of return, you give them full time to lead a team to go get this thing done, and you have active support of senior management, and that's what Six Sigma to us is all about."[26]

My point being that the statistical 'six standard deviations' aspect of Six Sigma is arguably not the main reason for its success as a transformational tool. Six Sigma is, in effect, shorthand for a management process that devotes significant executive time and dedicated resources to solving an organization's most significant problems – the problems that, if resolved, would deliver the most business value.

Six Sigma mania faded over time. Welch had tied employees' bonuses, promotions and stock options to Black Belt qualifications and achievements. People began to undertake Six Sigma projects just for the sake of it. Writing for *Quartz* magazine, financial journalist Oliver Saley spoke to one GE manager, who asked to remain anonymous. He reported that managers in sales departments complained about staff time lost to Six Sigma training, when the sales department itself drew little or no benefit from the process. "A growing number of Six Sigma projects launched by employees, essential for securing the all-important green belt, were no longer fixing major flaws in the company but instead focused on marginal, or even trivial, improvements," the article said. Staley also reported an unguarded comment made by Jeffrey Immelt, who took over as GE's CEO after Welch's retirement. On a 2016 call with investors and analysts, Immelt introduced a new initiative called 'additive manufacturing.' "If you put yourself in my shoes," he told the group, "additive manufacturing makes a shitload more sense than Six Sigma did. I was there the first day we did Six Sigma; it made no sense to me."[27] Additive manufacturing is a variant on 3-D printing.

It's a valuable technology, but it didn't prove to have Six Sigma's cult-like appeal.

Six Sigma evolved into Lean Six Sigma, an amalgamation of Lean Manufacturing and Six Sigma. As noted earlier, Lean itself grew out of the Toyota's vaunted TPS manufacturing and logistics approach, which originated in the 1940s. As Japan emerged from the devastation of World War II, Toyota was struggling to compete with giants like Ford.

The carmaker had begun life as the Toyoda Spinning and Weaving Company, founded in 1918 by inventor Sakichi Toyoda. Toyoda invented the world's first automatic loom, which would automatically stop if it detected a broken or missing thread, preventing wasteful production of faulty cloth. Toyoda's son, Kiichiro Toyoda, persuaded the company's board to move into automobile manufacturing after his father's death in 1930. The son had visited the US on business and saw that America's fledgling auto industry was booming, while loom manufacturers were in decline. In 1937, Toyoda's car business broke away from its parent company and renamed itself 'Toyota.' This was seen to have a more modern ring: the family name of Toyoda means 'fertile rice paddies,' which was felt to convey old-fashioned, agricultural vales.

After the war, competing with American manufacturers that were benefiting from massive economies of scale, Toyota had no option but to become more agile. As Jeffrey Liker writes in the preface to *The Toyota Way*, the company "made low volumes of multiple models of vehicles on the same production line. It kept inventories low, because it lacked storage space and could not afford to tie up cash in parts or finished vehicles. And it kept lead times short both in the procurement and utilization of parts and in the production and sale of vehicles. All of this lowered production costs and enabled Toyota to get cash fast and, in turn, to pay suppliers (which were also struggling financially) quickly."[28]

Writing in *Motor* magazine in 1938, Kiichiro Toyoda coined the magical words 'just in time.' "I plan to cut down on the slack time within work processes and in the shipping of parts and materials as much as possible," he wrote. "As the basic principle in realizing this plan, I will uphold the 'just in time' approach."[29] The three core principles that Toyoda introduced in his manufacturing plant were Just in Time (JIT); *jidoka* ('automation with human intelligence'), first introduced in the Toyoda automatic loom; and the standardization of processes.

Liker offers a nice definition of TPS. He describes it as a total 'living system.' "The goal is to produce a continual flow of value to the customer, without interruptions known as wastes."[30]

We referenced the three wastes that TPS seeks to eliminate in the previous chapter: *muda* ('waste,' or nonvalue-adding); *mura* (nonuniformity); and *muri* (overburdening). The concept of *muda* incorporates waste of all kinds: overproduction; time; movement; excess inventory; defective products; underused labour.

At the heart of the TPS philosophy is also the understanding that the world is constantly changing, and the resultant variation must be addressed by a culture of continuous improvement in the workplace.

There is much to admire in TPS, especially the way it embraces the humanity and intelligence of the workforce, asking for employees' constant input as to the efficiency of the process and encouraging innovation. There is a nice story told by auto executive John Krafcik, who invented the term 'lean production,' of a GM industrial engineer visiting the New United Motor Manufacturing Inc facility in California. As noted earlier, NUMMI was jointly owned by GM and Toyota, and used as an opportunity for a US plant to learn about TPS. The GM engineer asked a visiting Toyota executive how many industrial engineers worked at the plant – by which he meant how many 'managers' in the sense of the managers of Taylor's scientific management, devising the one best way to carry out a task and giving very specific instructions to the 'workers.' The Toyota executive thought for a time and then said, "We have 2,100 team members working on the factory floor; therefore, we have 2,100 industrial engineers."[31] In TPS, every worker is an industrial engineer.

Lean manufacturing was an important part of the 20th-century manufacturing landscape, and an element in what I am describing as the third phase of business transformation — a phase that can be said to include the quality movement.

In a paper titled, "Lean Six Sigma: yesterday, today and tomorrow," Jiju Antony, Ronald Snee and Roger Hoerl suggest that Lean Production and Six Sigma were both demonstrably successful methodologies whose key differences had the potential to be complementary. They noted that Six Sigma was focused on the use of data and statistical analysis to solve complex problems; Lean Production was based more on knowledge and experience, using tried-and-tested techniques to reduce waste and improve productivity. And Lean was not good at solving complex problems that required data and statistical analysis, while Six Sigma could be an overly complex tool for addressing relatively simple problems. They suggested that a mix of the two methodologies could be particularly effective. As the researchers noted, "Quality professionals found that Lean principles could be broadly and effectively applied with minimal data collection, and achieve immediate benefits. Then, for more complex problems requiring intense data analysis, Six Sigma could be utilized."[32]

Lean Six Sigma probably represents the apogee of the process management movement. It still has its adherents and practitioners, but the zeitgeist had moved on from ever-increasing efficiency. There is a straight line that can be drawn from Taylorism through ERP to Lean Six Sigma, but in a world increasingly driven by technology, Facebook founder Mark Zuckerberg's mantra of 'Move fast and break things' became more relevant: the next big breakthrough could be just around the corner; why waste time and money obsessively perfecting processes that were still being created? In the wider world of business, the lessons of process management had been learned, and the tools were readily available in the event that any established process needed to be streamlined.

What had the power to transform businesses was not process management, but insight. And insight would come from data. Lots of data.

5

THE FOURTH PHASE: DROWNING IN DATA LAKES

The big data revolution of the 21st century owes a great deal to the development of relational databases during the 1970s and '80s. The relational model of data was first proposed in 1970 by IBM computer scientist Edgar Codd, in a paper titled, "A Relational Model of Data for Large Shared Data Banks."[33] Codd's model was based on the idea of storing data in tables in which each row represents a record, and each column represents a field. Common keys that contain the same material in each table allow tables to be related to each other.

The relational model was a major breakthrough in database design. It provided a way to store and manage data in a way that was both efficient and easy to use. Prior to Codd's insights, computer databases were "completely ad hoc and higgledy-piggledy," as one of his former colleagues told *The New York Times*.[34] While "higgledy-piggledy" is not exactly a technical description, it gives a flavour of the significance of Codd's breakthrough.

Relational databases soon became the dominant type of database, and the proliferation of relational database management systems (RDBMSs) in the 1980s opened the door to new possibilities in data independence. RDBMSs were software applications that provided a user-friendly interface for creating, accessing and managing relational databases. Thanks to this technology, everyday users of data no longer had to know how and where the information was stored, or how the computer retrieved it. They could focus instead on how to put the data to use in their businesses.

The growth of the internet in the 1990s and early 2000s led to a huge increase in the amount of data that needed to be stored and managed. Relational databases were well suited to the task. Among other things, they provided a standard language for querying and analysing large volumes of data, called structured query language (SQL), and they could store and manage data for a wide variety of applications. But as the datasets grew from gigabytes to terabytes to petabytes, a more efficient means of storing and processing data beyond a single large computer was needed.

The next big breakthrough came in the form of Enter Apache Hadoop, a distributed file system and open-source processing framework designed to handle very large datasets across clusters of computers. Hadoop was originally developed by Doug Cutting and Mike Cafarella at Yahoo! in 2005 and named after Cutting's son's toy elephant.

Hadoop made it possible to break large datasets into smaller, bite-sized chunks, spread out across thousands of computers, allowing massive amounts of data to be analysed in parallel far more quickly. Hadoop has since become the de facto standard for big data processing and has further revolutionized database management. It has helped businesses unlock nonrelational enterprise data sources like weblogs, social media and point-of-sale devices.

Thanks to the growth of relational databases and technology like Hadoop, it became easier than ever for organizations to build and structure their own reservoirs of information. Soon, people were going crazy over data. Tech entrepreneurs and data enthusiasts started proclaiming that "data is the new oil." The first person to do so may have been Clive Humby, the British mathematician and data scientist behind the Tesco supermarket chain's Clubcard, who, according to *The Guardian* newspaper, coined the phrase back in 2006.[35] He was soon joined by a chorus of others. Meglena Kuneva, the European Consumer Commissioner, observed in 2009 that "[p]ersonal data is the new oil of the internet and the new currency of the digital world."[36] Gartner senior vice president Peter Sondergaard said in 2011 that "[i]nformation is the oil of the 21st century, and analytics is the combustion engine."[37]

It is entirely understandable that business came to believe that data was the answer. Companies around the world rushed to cash in on the data-oil craze. If data were the new oil, then, clearly, the more data the better. Developments in database technology and the cloud — something we take for granted today, but which was revolutionary in its day — drove businesses towards building 'data warehouses' and 'data lakes.' The two terms get used almost interchangeably, but they have different purposes and use different technologies. A data lake is a centralized repository for all data, regardless of its format or structure. It is designed to store data for long periods of time, and often used for exploratory data analysis and machine learning. A data warehouse, on the other hand, is a repository for structured data that has been cleaned and prepared for analysis. Data warehouses are designed to support business intelligence and reporting applications. They use what is called 'schema-on-load,' which requires analysts to design schema (structured outlines or frameworks) up front, before posing any queries. The analysts need to ask themselves questions beforehand — for instance, "What do these data tell me?" or "What do they describe?"— so they have a clear understanding of what's there and how they can use it.

Data lakes, in contrast, use what is called 'schema-on-use.' For instance, it might be decided that it would be useful to add data on the weather to a data lake, so at some point one could look at how weather conditions might play into something else that one wanted to explore. But data might be in Celsius or Fahrenheit. They might be recording the maximum temperature on a certain day, or the median temperature. This is simplistic, but it illustrates the problems faced by data analysts if someone wakes up one day and says, "Just pull down that weather data we uploaded."

Many companies committed to building such data lakes, believing that once the data was available, the business would figure out later how best to use it. Data vendors like Teradata and software companies like Oracle made a fortune creating and selling secured, managed clouds and other data management and analytics tools. At this stage, almost any source of data was considered a resource. The more the merrier. If you build the data lakes, it was thought, the insights will come. It became an obsession with some organizations: "We must get all our data together so we can access it in one place, and then we can dive in and pull out whatever we want."

One of the many barriers to effectively using these large data lakes was that there was often no context for different sets of data. Ideally, if you have a reservoir of data, somebody needs to own it. Someone needs to *curate* that data. They need to cherish it — maintain and improve it and ensure that it is representative and fit for purpose. But the IT departments were not experts in whatever the data represented. So, they would ask people in finance, or manufacturing, or sales, or HR to be responsible for 'their' data in the new data lake. These functions then became the custodians for their department's data. This created a new layer of administration and expense and, at a more funda-mental level, reinforced the central problem – that IT had assembled a huge amount of data that they didn't necessarily understand, and they had no sense of its practical business use. That in turn meant that they had no notion of the necessary quality threshold for the data. If data is to drive clear business decisions, there is a great deal of consensus on the level of data quality needed to be able to make the decisions. But because no one was sure what the data would be used for, it was impossible to set a meaningful quality threshold. There was only a notional level of data quality that nobody could be sure they had achieved. As a result, nobody was really in charge of the data lakes, and they were never ready to drink from. Maintaining these data lakes became increasingly expensive. They were turning into underutilized and poorly orchestrated money pits. And, inevitably, business executives became increasingly frustrated with IT.

As early as 2014, a Capgemini study found that only 27% of big data projects were regarded as success-ful, with just 13% of organizations claiming they had achieved full-scale production for their big data implementations.[38] Businesses were struggling with both the technical challenges of handling scattered silos of data and organizational hurdles, such as ineffective coordination among analytics teams. In 2017, Cisco reported that only 26% of its surveyed companies said they were successful with their 'internet of things' initiatives, with 60% saying that while "the initiatives look good on paper, [they] prove more complex than expected." Around the same time, Gartner estimated that about 60% of big data projects were failing. As noted earlier, Gartner soon reported that it was actually closer to 85%.[39] A 2019 Big Data and AI Executive Survey by NewVantage Partners provided further corroboration, with 77% of respondents reporting that the business adoption of big data initiatives was proving to be a major challenge.[40]

I still have regular conversations with business executives who tell me they are trying to work out how much their data is worth. I give them the same blunt answer: "Your data is worth nothing." It's a bit harsh, but unless you know what you can do with your data, all you are doing is wasting money managing it.

For the last 10 or 15 years, business leaders have been obsessed with big data, shelling out millions on building data lakes and data warehouses in the hope that "if we pool our data together, magical insights will arrive, and we'll all make money." It simply doesn't work like that. Apart from companies like Amazon and the cloud services businesses selling data solutions, which have done well from the supply of data management services, I fear that most organizations are in roughly the same position they were a decade ago. The fourth phase of business transformation has produced precious little transformation.

Many of the operational challenges with this approach to data stemmed from human problems, not technical failures. Despite announcing their move towards a data-first strategy, many senior executives didn't actually put the data first. They assigned the challenge to their IT teams, hoping they could simply capture data from everywhere and it would all blend together in beautiful harmony at some point in the future. In defence of IT departments the world over, data handling and data analytics sound like something you *should* give to the tech team, but most IT departments were given no meaningful business context for the task they were being charged with. IT teams, encouraged by vendors to buy cheap cloud-based storage, commissioned various different technologies to store data at scale. And off they went, capturing all the data they could.

In the next chapter, I'd like to explore the value-driven approach in more depth and look at the new, fifth phase of business transformation: insight-led and data-enabled.

I do fear that the fourth phase of business transformation— the dash for data — amounted to a lost decade in terms of business transformation. I'm not a huge fan of Six Sigma and the like, but the third phase, with its emphasis on disciplined process management, did unlock a great deal of business value. The era of data lakes has proved to be more of a money sink.

Hopefully, we have learned useful lessons along the way. I genuinely believe that the exciting new analytics technologies — AI, machine learning, natural language processing —have the power to harness the value that undoubtedly exists in data to truly transform our businesses.

THE
INTELLIGENCE
OF MACHINES

The pursuit of data lakes has led us on a long and expensive journey. The idea of pooling all your data in one place makes sense conceptually, but too often the process of creating the lake became the primary objective, rather than a focus on how to extract value from the data to drive outcomes in the business. The result is that you spend a lot of time and effort putting data in the lake, but you don't actually get to drink any water.

It doesn't have to be that way. Data is not just about technology. It is not "something the IT department should deal with." It is about driving outcomes from information and insight. The problem is not in the tooling. The tooling *is* fit for a purpose, and it changes at an ever-increasing pace. There are new developments, shortcuts, platforms and processes. The tooling is an IT issue; the business question is how you engage with and structure your consumption of the data and those services available within your organization. Once we have recognized the problem — that we have started from data up, when we needed to start from value down — we can restart the process properly. That means going back to the drivers of value for our businesses and deciding which insights, if generated from the available data, would produce the outcomes that deliver the best business results.

You will remember the DMAIC process from Six Sigma days (Define, Measure, Analyse, Improve, Control) and how we said that the initial 'Define' element was probably the most significant reason for the success of Six Sigma. The process demanded that senior executives choose the aspects of the business that had the most potential to deliver results if they were fixed or changed, and that leadership stick with the change programmes that were implemented as a result.

But Six Sigma was essentially a process of improvement: defects reduced; costs reduced; processes streamlined. Insight-led, data-enabled transformation gives us the opportunity to completely reimagine our businesses.

Once we understand the question, we can look for relevant data that might deliver a solution and let data analytics loose on the newly assembled dataset to see if an answer can be found. If those data don't provide the answer, move on and look for new data. Fail fast. Move quickly. These early stages of the process are risk-free, in a very real sense, because the experimentation takes place in the virtual world of data.

This 'value down' approach forces us to identify what we want to achieve, the questions we need to ask, and the hypotheses we can formulate around those questions that will allow us to test them, to see if they deliver. Once we have articulated those, we can identify which elements from all the available data, either owned, acquired or open, will help us to validate those hypotheses. Can I find those data? Are they appropriately described? Are they of the right level of quality? Can they deliver on the desired outcome?

When this becomes the basic template for our operating model, we can add scope to it. We can simply add another dataset or another problem to it. But now, we have a blueprint for exploring and answering business problems, above and beyond the 'boil the ocean' approach represented by most data lakes. Data will not magically provide us with answers. There is no mysterious algorithm that can be turned loose on a mass of undifferentiated data to produce a meaningful business answer. We have to decide what business problems it would be most valuable to solve — the heart of the Six Sigma approach — and then look for the data that might hold the answer, and the analytic methodology that might be able to unlock those data.

* * *

I hope it has become clear at this point in the book that when I talk about 'interrogating the data' in the search for added value, I am talking about data analytics techniques that make use of various forms of AI: machine learning, natural language processing, computer vision and the like. So, it is probably time to explore what we mean, and don't mean, by artificial intelligence and key technologies like machine learning.

It's a shame that we ever started to use the term artificial *intelligence*, because it unnecessarily raises the philosophical question of "What do we meant by intelligence?" There is a lot of interesting history behind what we now call AI, which we'll discuss in a moment. The key point is that when we talk about AI in the context of data analytics, we are not talking about 'Artificial General Intelligence' (AGI), also known as 'strong' or 'deep' AI. The term AGI denotes AI with a human-level intelligence that is capable of consciousness and self-awareness. This was actually the goal of the first researchers into AI, because they couldn't imagine any form of intelligence that wasn't intelligent in the human sense. And for humans, the concept of intelligence is unavoidably linked to the idea of consciousness, leading to concerns that any form of artificial intelligence would also be sentient, and possibly more concerned about its own survival than ours. In reality, this is still in the realm of science fiction, as in *The Terminator*, where a superintelligent system called Skynet becomes self-aware and turns on its human creators.

Such existential fears are understandable and have been a part of the conversation surrounding AI since the earliest days of the technology. In the 1940s, the Hungarian-American mathematician John von Neuman worried that humans would soon find themselves unable to keep pace with their AI creations. Von Neuman envisioned a future in which the AI 'automata' created by humans followed an 'explosive' development trajectory in which they themselves began to create new and even more intelligent machines. These new creations, he imagined, would soon become capable of operations beyond human comprehension. At this point, humans would have lost control. They would no longer understand the technology of the new machines, so they wouldn't be able to stop them doing whatever they might be doing, even if it was harmful to human beings. Von Neumann called the point in the future at which such technological advances became intractable and irreversible the 'technological singularity.'

These concerns continue to animate the discussion about AI. University of Oxford philosopher Nick Bostrom argued in his 2014 book, *Superintelligence*, that there is good reason to believe that through our AI and neuroscientific endeavours we will find ourselves on the brink of creating a true superintelligence in the next few decades.[41] This superintelligent entity could take the form of a human brain enhanced with machine interfaces, or a 'whole brain emulation' in which a neural network fully models the physical structure of the brain, or perhaps some form of web-based cognitive system like a superintelligent internet. Bostrom thinks that some form of superintelligence will be devised in the not-too-distant future, and he recognizes the incredible potential behind the expanding technology. But he also raises concerns about the point when a superintelligent entity surpasses the frontiers of human intelligence and understanding. Bostrom calls this launching point the entity's 'takeoff,' and he sketches out the possible timeframes for such a development. In 'fast takeoff scenarios,' for example, the superintelligent entity improves its own capabilities before humans have time to work out what to do about the possible undesirable side effects — such as the new entity deciding to devote all of the world's energy resources to its own continued survival.

The good news is that we remain a long way from creating an AGI with the capabilities of human intelligence. Michael Kanaan, the first US Air Force Chairperson for Artificial Intelligence and former Director of Operations for the USAF-MIT Artificial Intelligence Accelerator, is a pretty hard-headed guy. In his book, *T-Minus AI*, he says that it's important to understand that "neither artificial general intelligence (AGI) nor superintelligence is within the reach or even the possible range of current AI design, or any currently known technology."[42] So let's go with Kanaan for now.

The AI technology that we are concerned with in this book is already here. We encounter it every day. AI recommends songs on our streaming apps, drives our online searches, decides which posts, news items and advertisements to serve us on social media, guides our in-car navigation systems and autocompletes our email messages. AI technology already possesses many human-like cognitive abilities, but it doesn't have 'general intelligence,' and it is not sentient.

The term artificial intelligence was coined in 1955 by Dartmouth College mathematics professor John McCarthy, in a funding application to the Rockefeller Foundation for a summer research project. In the now-historic proposal, McCarthy and his colleagues — Marvin Minksy of Harvard, Nathaniel Rochester from IBM and Claude Shannon from Bell Telephone Laboratories, all now considered founding figures in computer science and AI research — pitched a modest "two-month, 10-man study of artificial intelligence." The stated intent was to explore the hypothesis "that every aspect of learning or any other feature of intelligence can in principle be so precisely described that a machine can be made to simulate it."[43] The proposal resulted in a gathering of computer scientists at Dartmouth the following year that would launch the new field of study and pave the way for decades of important research into what would thereafter be known as artificial intelligence.

The idea of describing human intelligence in logical or 'symbolic' terms underpinned these early explorations of what is now called 'Good Old-Fashioned Artificial Intelligence' (GOFAI). In the same way that symbolic logic had proved able to turn 'logical thought' into a series of symbols, axioms and rules of inference that would allow what had previously seemed to be a quintessentially human process into a series of mathematical formulae, there was an understandable belief that all of human thought could, in principle, be described in essentially mathematical terms, in a way that a machine could be programmed to deal with. It turned out that this was not the best way forward for what we now call AI, and it took a lot more than the McCarthy proposal's 'two months and 10 men' to figure that out. There have been two major 'AI Winters' since the Dartmouth gathering — periods when faith in the possibility of developing useful forms of AI wavered, with a subsequent decline in funding.

One of the seminal thinkers on the subject of machine intelligence was Alan Turing, the famed British computer scientist. In his landmark article, 'Computing machinery and intelligence,' published in *Mind* in 1950, Turing posed the central question: "Can machines think?" But he argued that this was a 'meaningless' question. "May not machines carry out something which ought to be described as thinking," he asked, "but which is very different from what a man does?" If a machine was capable of demonstrating or simulating intelligent behaviour, Turing argued, then we shouldn't be too concerned about whether it was thinking, in a human sense, especially since we can't really explain what we mean by 'thinking.' We know that we ourselves think and (unless we are solipsists) we infer that other people are probably thinking as well. Or maybe not. So why (paraphrasing Turing a bit radically) should we bother ourselves about whether a machine is 'thinking?' And how would we ever know? Imitating intelligence to a sufficient degree should be enough for us to accept that the machine was behaving 'intelligently.'

To test whether a machine was capable of a level of intelligence that was indistinguishable from human thinking, Turing proposed what he called the 'Imitation Game.' A human interrogator poses questions to a machine. The answers given by the machine might be generated by a human or by the machine. If the interrogator can't tell whether the respondent is human or not from its responses, the machine has passed what we now call the Turing test. "I believe that at the end of the century," Turing wrote, "the use of words and general educated opinion will have altered so much that one will be able to speak of machines thinking without expecting to be contradicted."[44] It may have taken a little longer than 'the end of the century', but that was a prescient statement.

I typed "What is the Turing test?" into Microsoft's new AI-driven search engine, Bing AI, and this was the machine's response: "The Turing test is a test of a machine's ability to exhibit intelligent behaviour equivalent to, or indistinguishable from, that of a human. It was proposed by Alan Turing in 1950. The test involves a human evaluator who judges natural language conversations between a human and a machine designed to generate human-like responses. If the machine can engage in a conversation with a human without being detected as a machine, it has demonstrated human intelligence." I can't tell if Bing AI's response was written by a machine. Maybe Microsoft has an army of real people at its HQ in Redmond, Washington, frantically typing the answers to everyone's questions and pinging them back to us. But I don't think so. Bing AI passes the Turing test. Alan Turing would argue that we might as well say that the machine is 'intelligent.'

* * *

During World War II, Turing spent time at Bell Labs in New York City and met Shannon, one of the key participants in McCarthy's Dartmouth project. The two great minds discussed the possibilities of machine intelligence at length, including whether it would be possible to create a computer program that could compete at chess with human players. Chess was popular among computer scientists and had long been seen as the epitome of human thinking and intelligence. Both Turing and Shannon developed early computer chess-playing programs in the 1950s to explore the capabilities of AI.

Chess-playing programs gradually, and then quickly, improved to the point where they could challenge even the most gifted human players, culminating with the epic showdown between grandmaster Garry Kasparov and IBM's 'Deep Blue' computer program in 1997. Capturing the public mood, *Newsweek* ran a cover with the headline, "The Brain's Last Stand." A possible victory by a computer against a human grandmaster was seen as an existential threat to humanity's perception of itself as the most intelligent entity on Earth, and possibly the universe. Backed by an algorithm developed by a team of computer scientists and engineers, with the help of chess grandmasters, Deep Blue was capable of 200 million calculations per second. It was good enough to beat Kasparov in a six-game series that Deep Blue won 3.5 to 2.5. It was a devastating loss for the so-called 'best player of all time,' but a significant moment in the development of artificial intelligence programs.

Kasparov felt despondent after the loss and even accused IBM of cheating. He had made an unusual move, attacking Deep Blue's knight, a move he was convinced would lead the computer to retreat. Instead, Deep Blue sacrificed its knight. "Machines are not speculative attackers," wrote Kasparov in his book, *Deep Thinking*. He had discussed the move (in Russian) with his team at New York's Plaza Hotel and feared they had been overheard by a Russian-speaking 'spy' planted by the IBM team and masquerading as hotel staff. A clearly preposterous and paranoid idea, right? But Kasparov later learned that IBM had programmed Deep Blue to respond as it did on the very morning of the final game. Which is enough to make any grandmaster just a little bit paranoid.

Kasparov grew more reflective as the years passed and acknowledged the inevitable and overwhelming pace of AI development. "The depressing truth is that a few years and a new generation of faster chips later, none of it would have mattered very much," he observed.

"For better or worse, chess just wasn't deep enough to force the chess-machine community to find a solution beyond speed, something many among them lamented."[45]

Deep Blue was able to search quickly through a vast database of potential moves and apply them according to certain pre-set parameters. It was an impressive feat, but it wasn't necessary for the computer to be 'intelligent' in the human sense. The AI used to develop Deep Blue required human experts to program the machine with the rules of the game, load the database of potential moves, and construct the set of 'if-then' rules that would ultimately guide the expert system to victory. Deep Blue was an incredibly fast, sophisticated, well-trained machine.

One of the key facets of modern AI's evolution has been the development of machine learning, the process by which a program's reliance on 'expert' human input is removed and it teaches itself how to achieve a desired result.

The concept of machine learning first emerged in the 1950s. The term was coined by IBM's Arthur Samuel, a pioneering computer scientist who developed the first self-learning computer program to play another board game: checkers. In a 1959 paper, 'Some Studies in Machine Learning Using the Game of Checkers,' Samuel laid out procedures by which a computer program could learn "to play a better game of checkers than can be played by the person who wrote the program."[46] The aim was to enable a computer program to learn how to improve its own performance of a particular task based on its own prior experiences.

This type of learning was modelled on the human brain's learning architecture, through the development of artificial neural networks (ANNs). The nodes of the ANNs were designed to behave like neurons in the human brain, which receive signals from sense perceptions or other neurons and transmit an electrochemical pulse in proportion to the activation potential created along their membranes. This pulse, in turn, excites or inhibits activity in other connected neurons.

The basic unit of an ANN is the node. Like a neuron in the human brain, each node has a number of inputs and a single output. The inputs are connected to the node by a weighting hierarchy, which determines how much influence each input has on the 'total input' of the node. The nodes are also arranged in hidden layers. The input layer of an ANN is where the data is entered into the network. The intermediary layers are where the data is processed and transformed. The output layer is where the results of the processing are outputted. The outgoing signal produced by a node may be proportional to the weighted total input, the result of a specified mathematical function, or correspond to a pre-set threshold so that it only sends an output when the total input passes a certain value.

Like networks of neurons, networks of artificial nodes can be trained to produce specific outputs, given the inputs of data they have received. The inputs are weighted and combined to produce a single output, with the weighting being adjusted over time to produce more accurate results. A 'training set' of data can be fed into the network so that the weightings and connections between the nodes can be adjusted to produce a desired output. An ANN in a self-driving car program might be trained, for example, to recognize stop signs through the use of a large training set of stop sign images, taken in a variety of traffic situations and weather conditions. The network can learn to recognize a stop sign in the way a human brain can, and ultimately produce the correct output signal to stop the vehicle upon recognition of that input.

One of the first algorithms to demonstrate machine learning was known as the 'perceptron,' which used supervised learning to classify visual input data and recognise rudimentary images. Developed at the Cornell Aeronautical Laboratory in 1958 by the psychologist Dr Frank Rosenblatt, the perceptron was based on the idea of a neuron, with each neuron having multiple inputs and a single output. It was an early version of an ANN, and it immediately prompted predictions that the perceptron would eventually become self-aware. "The Navy revealed the embryo of an electronic computer that it believes will be able to walk, talk, see, write, reproduce itself and be conscious of its existence," a 1958 article in *The New York Times* proclaimed. Rosenblatt was quoted saying that the machine would be "the first device to think as the human brain."

Such fears about that particular machine and consciousness were misplaced, but Rosenblatt and others were correct about the technology's potential. Intermediate layers of interconnected nodes were later added to Rosenblatt's original three layers of nodes in the perceptron, allowing more complex operations and more sophisticated outputs. These more advanced networks were called 'deep' neural networks. The fundamental concept of weighted inputs and outputs in a network of connected nodes became known as 'connectionism,' and formed the basis of many of the core techniques used in modern machine learning.

In practice, this trial-and-error approach of adjusting weighting to deliver a desired output (such as the matching of visual images) seemed unfeasibly complex, and as some researchers argued against the core logic of the approach, funding and interest in the AI field collapsed, leading to a decade-long 'connectionist winter.' Research in general switched back to a focus on symbolic AI (GOFAI).

Other researchers, such as the British-Canadian cognitive psychologist and computer scientist Geoffrey Hinton, kept working on the refinement of neural networks. In the 1980s, Hinton, along with David Rumelhart and Ronald Williams of the University of California, San Diego, developed what was called the 'backpropagation algorithm.' It was an attempt to overcome the limitations of the perceptron by allowing ANNs to 'teach themselves' to classify more complex datasets. The backpropagation algorithm works by comparing the actual output of the network to the desired output, and adjusting the weighting of the network until it gets the result it wants. It's essentially a brilliant way of automating the process of trial and error by which human beings trained the earliest networks, and it underpins the whole of machine learning.

The backpropagation algorithm immediately opened up the possibility that computers could learn things that humans had been unable to program them to do using GOFAI. One of the tasks that had eluded symbolic AI researchers was language translation. Attempts had been made to teach machines the rules of syntax and grammar, to allow them to generate sentences with the same meaning in another language, but such sets of rules proved incapable of capturing the vagaries of human language. As one (probably apocryphal) story goes, the English sentence, "The spirit is willing, but the flesh is weak," might be translated into the Russian sentence "The vodka is good, but the meat is rotten."

In the late 1980s, IBM's Thomas J Watson Research Center in Yorktown Heights, New York, began experimenting with a machine translation system that essentially taught itself to convert from one language to another by being given an enormous number of examples of texts that had already been translated by humans. When fed a new piece of text (or 'string') in one language, the machine would search its database for the string in the target language that had the highest probability of being a correct translation.

The system was based on statistical techniques and had first been proposed in the 1940s, at a time when there were not enough computer resources available for the approach to be tested. In 1988, IBM started a project known as Candide, using transcripts of the proceedings of the Canadian Parliament, which are recorded in both English and French. The research team fed more than two million pairs of sentences from these records into their computer. The results were far from perfect, but hopeful enough to suggest that statistical techniques had real potential for language translation. In 2007, Google switched from SYSTRAN, one of the oldest rule-based machine translation technologies, to its own statistical learning system. The growing power of machine learning networks was driven to a great extent by the availability of increasingly large datasets.

The growth of the internet and the use of smartphones over the past few decades have fuelled an explosion of data. A 2002 study by the University of California, Berkeley, estimated that the total amount of data produced in print, film, magnetic tape and earlier forms of media worldwide was around 5 exabytes (5 billion gigabytes) at the time.[47] By 2020, according to the International Data Center, the amount of data produced worldwide had reached over 64 zettabytes (64 trillion gigabytes), representing a 20,000-fold growth since 2002.[48] The availability of such a large amount of data has also breathed new life into previously developed algorithms that were thought to be useless or outdated. "You can take one of those simple machine-learning algorithms that you learned about in the first few weeks of an AI class," Joe Estelle, a software engineer for Google Translate, told *The Atlantic* magazine in 2013, "an algorithm that academia has given up on, that's not seen as useful — but when you go from 10,000 training examples to 10 billion training examples, it all starts to work. Data trumps everything."[49]

With more data available in digital form than ever before, ANNs proved capable of delivering even more impressive feats than the AI systems of just a decade earlier. This included more advanced gameplay.

IBM's Deep Blue had beaten Garry Kasparov at chess, but the ancient game of Go represented an even more complex challenge for computer programs. Go is an abstract strategy board game for two players that originated in Asia more than 2,500 years ago. It is played on a 19x19 grid of black and white squares, with each player having 181 stones of their own colour. The goal is simple: to expand one's territory and occupy a larger total area of the board. But the number of possible moves is mind-boggling — the number of potential board positions, calculated at approximately 2.1×10^{170} is greater than the number of atoms in the universe. (The number of possible moves in a typical game of chess is 'only' $10.^{120}$)

A London-based company called DeepMind Technologies developed a program called AlphaGo that uses sophisticated machine learning techniques to play the game. The company was headed by entrepreneur Demis Hassabis, a chess prodigy who had taught himself to program as a boy and been accepted to the University of Cambridge at age 16. To win at Go, Hassabis and his fellow AlphaGo developers used a deep neural network to analyse gameplay options and potential moves based on the best expected outcome. The programmers initially trained it by downloading the records of more than 100,000 online games played by talented human competitors. From that foundation, AlphaGo improved and refined its strategy by playing more than 30 million games against itself and analysing its own moves.

In October 2015, AlphaGo became the first computer program to beat a human professional Go player, and the following year DeepMind invited the world Go champion, South Korean Lee Sedol, to a match. The contest, held at the Four Seasons Hotel in Seoul, caught the world's attention in the same way Kasparov's matches against Deep Blue once had. And, like Kasparov, Lee was quickly humbled by his digital opponent's skill. Halfway through the first game, AlphaGo made a particularly unorthodox move that made Lee's jaw literally drop. He subsequently lost the match. In the second game, AlphaGo made a move (move 37) that commentators described as "totally unthinkable." Again, Lee was forced to concede. He won the next two games, but ultimately lost the five-game series 3-2, in a landmark victory for artificial intelligence. Lee was gracious in defeat. "I would like to express my respect to the programmers for making such an amazing program," he said. He also said that he'd assumed AlphaGo would be based on "'probability calculation," but found its unexpected and "unthinkable" move to be truly creative. AlphaGo had found ways of winning that human players had not considered. "What surprised me the most," said Lee, "was that [Alpha Go] showed us that moves humans may have thought are creative were actually conventional."

After the defeat of Sedol, the DeepMind team went on to develop AlphaGo Zero, a program that taught itself to play Go from scratch, without any initial 'supervised training' in the form of datasets of games played by humans. In an experiment by the team, a 'self-taught' program defeated a version of itself that had been trained on human games. It seemed that the machine was developing superior strategies when left to its own devices, as Sedol had suggested.

Machine learning has grown in scope over the past decade. Today's machine learning algorithms can be classified into three broad groups: 'supervised learning,' in which an algorithm learns from example data that it is fed to help it learn; 'unsupervised learning,' in which an algorithm learns to deliver a desired result by recognizing patterns in sets of data given to it; and 'reinforcement learning,' in which algorithms are presented with example data, accompanied by positive or negative feedback, so that their decisions have consequences. This represents a highly sophisticated means of learning by trial and error.

Machine learning applications are now capable of complex tasks. Two of the most transformational applications are natural language processing and computer vision technologies.

Natural language processing drives voice-controlled assistants like Siri and Alexa, and translation algorithms such as Google Translate. Advances in this domain have been moving quickly and making headlines. OpenAI's ChatGPT (Generative Pretrained Transformer), a natural language processing tool driven by AI technology, has been trained on massive datasets of text drawn from the internet and is capable of generating human-like text responses. Computer vision (CV) uses ANNs to process, analyse and interpret visual data, allowing computers or electronic devices to distinguish and identify objects, people or images, enabling facial recognition and a wide range of other visual applications, such as scanning medical images to detect signs of disease or analysing images of the interior of pipelines to detect cracks. Those initial predictions of what the early 'perceptron' might be able to accomplish now seem more prescient than fanciful.

NOT ALL
DATA ARE
CREATED
EQUAL

The fifth phase of business transformation will be insight-led and data-enabled, and driven by the astonishing power of AI technologies.

We need to move from a data-driven, 'data up' approach to a value-driven, 'value down' approach. One of the problems with the whole concept of data lakes is that they work on the assumption that all datasets have equal value. But all data are not equal. Data in itself has no value. But a set of data that has no apparent inherent value may have the potential to become extremely valuable when linked to other sets of data and viewed through the lens of value.

Business leaders need to frame the questions that have the potential to add real value to their businesses. I find it useful to see any business as a series of potential optimization points, and then work out which individual optimization has the capacity to deliver most added value. The goal is to produce a 'value map' of the organization. Very often, the optimization points that have the most value occur throughout the various silos of the organization. Making a radical improvement to the optimization point can ripple through the whole organization, adding surprising amounts of new value. The trick is to 'test' this optimization, to create a 'proof of value.' That is, to prove that we have the ability to make the improvement we want, and the improvement will deliver the desired added value.

The concept of proof of value is distinct from the usual understanding of 'proof of concept' in business. Very few proofs of concept break genuinely new ground. They tend to apply established techniques to a business problem in the appropriate order, and with the right structure, to achieve a desired outcome. The focus tends to be more on whether the solution will actually work than on whether it will deliver real value. With proof of *value*, the focus is on testing small-scale but valid scenarios to see if they not only work but also deliver real value. Embarrassingly large numbers of data projects have consumed huge amounts of money and failed to deliver significant value. Sometimes they fail to work at all and are abandoned.

Proof of value is an experimental, agile process. A key part of the agile approach is to constantly review progress, and to assess blockers and barriers using the mantra, 'pause, pivot or stop.' At each barrier to progress we decide whether to pause, while we look for new data, or perhaps an enhancement, that would allow us to then move ahead. Or, pivot and approach the problem from an entirely different angle. Or, stop and agree that this approach doesn't seem to be working.

In this second part of this book, I will focus on real-life examples of insight-led and data-enabled business transformation, because this is first and foremost a practical approach. The fifth phase of business transformation is all about driving value from data and using the power of AI to generate new insights.

* * *

I worked with a major high street retailer whose business was hard hit by the COVID-19 pandemic. It had a negligible online presence, was entirely dependent on footfall, and it was severely impacted by the sudden and dramatic fall-off in the number of people physically visiting stores to do their shopping. The problem was compounded by the fact that the chain had always relied on revenue predictions to set store-by-store staffing levels. It wasn't rocket science, but it worked. Each store historically had quite predictable fluctuations in sales, following seasonal patterns, as well as shorter-term daily or weekly fluctuations. They would plan staffing for each store accordingly, adjusting the roster of part-time workers eight weeks in advance to ensure optimum coverage and fulfil their commitments to part-time employees, who were not on zero-hour contracts. Levels of full-time staff were adjusted based on store revenue; a location that was showing a steady increase in revenues would gradually staff up.

With the onset of the pandemic, revenues for all stores declined dramatically, but also began to fluctuate dramatically and unpredictably, due to a combination of local circumstances that no one yet understood. Before the pandemic, they had been able to use historical data to forecast store revenue with a high degree of accuracy: around 85%. When we looked at the revenue data during the pandemic, one of the data scientists described the figures she was seeing as 'anti-pattern.' They were apparently random, or 'stochastic,' as the data scientists say. It had become impossible to predict the future.

Our first thought was to abandon historic revenue trends and look at some form of current data that might tell what was actually happening in something like real time. We decided to look at footfall around every store, to try and determine how many people were in the vicinity at any given time, and then see if the accuracy of that data allowed us to estimate how many walked past versus how many crossed the threshold into the store.

There are providers who aggregate data from mobile phone apps to give the exact location of phone users, accurate to within eight square metres. Many apps ask for access to phone users' location — weather apps, maps, timetable services, some games, etc. The data obtained are anonymous, of course, and subject to relevant government oversight — such as the General Data Protection Regulation (GDPR) guidelines in Europe — but enough people have their location enabled to provide a remarkably accurate picture of where large numbers of a country's inhabitants are at any moment in time. It is sufficiently accurate to show whether they are outside a particular store, or inside.

We bought a sample of the data for the postcodes of a set of stores and tested it. In heavily populated areas, the data were quite strong, but in more rural areas, the numbers were too low to be statistically viable.

I tell this part of the story — which isn't all that dramatic — to make the point that you can never be certain which data may offer the insight you are seeking. It is rather remarkable that there are data available that can geolocate large numbers of people with that degree of specificity, but in this instance, the data were not remarkable enough. Which goes to my point that most data lakes are full of data that may or may not provide the answers we are looking for, and maintaining those lakes at considerable expense may or may not be a sound investment.

At this point, we did a pivot and went back to the only hard data we had, which was actual revenue data. What we did, in simple terms, was turn up the sensitivity of the analysis. When you have strong historical trends, you tend to suppress the response to what may be anomalies. If you are looking at a nice, long curve on a graph that shows a clear, long-term pattern, you 'zoom out' to see the picture, and can afford to ignore fluctuations that would be visible if you were to zoom in. We zoomed in. We built a high-velocity pipeline of the company's trading data so that we were capturing every store's hourly proceeds on a daily basis, and importing that into our model every week. We would then run a new forecast based on what we had learned from that week's data. If we saw a drop in one store's revenues, we lowered our expectations. If there was an uptick, we raised them.

We then factored in any measure we could turn to that would reflect the obvious externalities that were affecting, or would affect, store traffic and revenue, such as the level of pandemic-related government restriction on movement that was or was expected to be in place at any time. We also factored in competitor density, on the assumption that if there were not many people shopping in the first place, and there were several options for them to buy what they wanted, the effect on individual store's trade would be exacerbated. This was another example of 'zooming in' — in normal times, the effect of having one or more competitors nearby would be a constant factor, absorbed into the longer-term trends. If, however, there are only 10 shoppers on the high street at a given time, and they have three places where they can buy the same thing, the effect will be more dramatic.

The model used statistical and deep learning techniques to find patterns in what had seemed to be stochastic data. In the end, we were able to create an hourly forecast of transactions for every store, for every trading hour, projecting out eight weeks ahead, with sufficient accuracy to allow the retailer to plan their staffing levels.

The moral of this tale, I would suggest, is in the 'pivot.' We assumed that the amazing phone app data (known in the trade as 'mobility' data) would solve the problem. We could have plunged in and bought a load of mobility data, but we bought a sample and tested it to see if it would deliver the insight we wanted. And it wouldn't. In the end, some surprisingly heavyweight AI techniques proved able to make a reliable forecast from a very sparse amount of the usual data, overlaid with a number of factors that attempted to mirror the effect pandemic restrictions were having on the high street.

Accumulating all the data in the world in the hope that they provide some as-yet unspecified insight is not the way forward. Again, we need to decide what insights have the potential to deliver the most value, and test different datasets to be certain they have the capability to deliver the insight we need.

Another interesting example in this context was a project undertaken some time ago for the UK's Forestry Commission.

The government agency's primary responsibility is to maintain the country's stock of trees. It does this by managing existing woodlands and forests and planting new trees on public land. It also provides subsidies to private landowners to grow trees on their property and monitors this land to ensure compliance. The commission also relies on public goodwill as a source of information on things like illegal felling and storm damage. Timber can be salvaged from recently fallen trees, but one that lies on the forest floor too long quickly decays and become worthless. Major storms can bring down trees worth hundreds of millions of pounds. Illegal fellers tend to operate away from roads, where they won't be seen by the general public. And it's not unheard of for landowners who are receiving subsidies to only plant trees around the edges of a piece of land, giving the impression that a larger area has been planted.

The vast amount of woodland and the Forestry Commission's limited resources and staffing mean that less than 10% of all sites could be feasibly monitored in a given year through on-site inspections. Monitoring relies on a combination of physical inspection and aerial photography, as well as, in recent years, satellite imagery. Aerial photography is expensive and would be commissioned only infrequently; satellite imagery is cheaper but can be affected by cloud cover. Reviewing images created by aerial or satellite photography was a painstaking job requiring the visual comparison of a recent image of, say, a 50-square-metre area of land with a similar image taken perhaps six months earlier. If the most recent image was affected by cloud cover, the exercise was futile.

But there was a potential alternative source of data. Imagery known as Synthetic Aperture Radar (SAR) data is generated when a sensor on an orbiting satellite transmits electromagnetic signals towards the Earth's surface and receives bounced-back signals. The satellite measures the time it takes for the signals to travel from the sensor to the surface and back, and uses this to create a crude two-dimensional image of the Earth's surface. SAR data are not impacted by cloud cover, and the measurements are taken frequently (approximately every five days). The black-and-white backscatter plots lack the refinement of optical imagery, but we thought that, with auxiliary data sources, perhaps machine learning programs could be trained to use SAR data to distinguish levels of tree cover.

This was essentially a computer vision problem, taking the kinds of techniques involved in facial recognition, for example, and applying them to the surface of the planet. The task was made more challenging by the fact that the data were coming from satellites moving at high speeds around a rotating planet that has varying types of terrain, like mountains and valleys.

Two years of raw SAR data were downloaded and processed to eliminate any signal noise and make adjustments for distortion due to the tilt of satellite sensors or variations in the terrain. Auxiliary data from the Forestry Commission were used to set the 'ground truth' baseline on which the machine learning model would be trained.

In this case, the proof-of-value exercise was very successful. The Forestry Commission said that after two weeks, they were being told things it had previously taken 30 years to learn, and that after four weeks they were being told things they'd never known.

Satellite technology has moved on since the time of this project, and it's now possible to take images that penetrate cloud cover, and AI is routinely used to analyse images. The days of researchers poring over desks covered with photographs is long gone. But it was groundbreaking at the time, and is another example of how unexpected data sources — SAR data, in this case — may be able to deliver the insight we seek.

There are other examples of using AI to harvest new insights. Sometimes, the type of data you need for analysis is already being captured by your business, but not in a form that will solve the problem you have. We once did some work for a major soft drinks manufacturer, looking at one of their bottling plants in the Netherlands. The facility was experiencing frequent breakdowns and delays, and operating well below its theoretical capacity.

The machines on the bottling line were controlled by mini-computers called programmable logic controllers (PLCs). These devices have little in the way of onboard memory and are not typically networked, but they do have a component known as an 'historian.' This records a history of machine errors for up to the preceding seven days, before the memory is full and the error history is recorded over.

In theory, this record of errors — including the timing, type of error and frequency of error — is just the sort of data source that could provide us with the raw information necessary to work out primary causes of the factory line's problems. But because the data being collected by the PLCs were effectively getting deleted every week, there wasn't enough to conduct an effective analysis of the error history. One week's data would capture perhaps one significant failure, but it wouldn't allow a deeper analysis to reveal the subtle combination of events that were leading to frequent breakdowns over time. The PLCs were upgraded to be able to collect several months of data, and machine-learning techniques were then able to reveal the pattern of issues behind what turned out to be a complex chain of events. We then had a picture of 'if this, and this, and this, then that, but only if....' The plant was collecting the right data, but there just wasn't enough of it.

It is hard — perhaps impossible — to know in advance exactly what data will give us the insight we need to solve our future problems. The answer is not to collect and hoard every imaginable piece of data, just in case it at some point gives us the answer we need. The key is to identify the insight we need and then test data from all available sources, to see if they have the potential to deliver.

LEAVING THE TOOL-O-SPHERE

Business transformation is not a technical issue, it's a business issue. This will require leaders to think and act differently. Rather than seeing data as operational, they need to view them as an enabler for real business transformation. They will need to constantly articulate big, valuable questions and identify the insights that have the potential to drive value.

The biggest challenge to achieving genuinely transformational results is that many businesses struggle to support changes that go beyond the sphere of normal business. It is much easier to improve an existing business practice (as in the third phase of business transformation, process management) than it is to consider running that business in a radically different way.

A few years ago, Jonathan Gifford and I coauthored *My Steam Engine Is Broken*. The subtitle of the book was '*Taking the organization from the industrial era to the age of ideas,*' and the core argument was that many, and arguably most, modern organizations are effectively stuck in the industrial era, using work and management structures that would be instantly recognizable to Frederick Winslow Taylor more than 100 years ago. In the second chapter of this book, I applauded Taylor for bringing scientific thinking to the world of business: forming new hypotheses about how things might be done in different and better ways, and testing these to show which offered the best solution in practice. But the science has moved on. We now have the capability to interrogate our businesses with tools that are light years away from the old 'time and motion' study.

There was a metaphor at the heart of *My Steam Engine Is Broken*, which came from a time when I was designing and delivering leadership development programmes at Oxford University's Saïd Business School. I encouraged leaders to see the world differently, and think the unthinkable, by engaging them with a wide range people who worked in the arts: painters, actors, directors, storytellers, poets, conductors and dancers. What became obvious to me was that the leaders were perfectly capable of change. I saw a number of them go through quite profound changes. Some decided to leave their jobs and set out in entirely new directions, which was an interesting but unintended consequence. Most would experience some particular epiphany — a moment when an artist or a dancer or a poet would strike some chord with them, and they would suddenly *get it*. They would see the world from a different perspective, and realize how that new point of view could add real value to their business leadership.

But when I would talk with these leaders again in follow-up conversations, it was apparent that most would return to their companies brimming with exciting new ideas ... and nothing would happen. Nothing would change. The organization would listen politely, nod and smile, and carry on exactly as it always had. I came to feel that it was like training generals in the tactics and techniques of 21st-century warfare, with the leadership equivalent of the most modern military hardware and technology and cutting-edge battlefield tactics. They would go away ready to engage in 21st-century warfare, and the organization would put them back in the trenches, pointing proudly at the new Lewis light machine gun that troops were being given as proof that they were running a genuinely modern army.

The metaphor at the heart of that earlier book was, of course, the steam engine itself. Too many modern businesses are the organizational equivalent of the great steam engines of the late 19th and early 20th centuries, and they have decided to keep repairing the creaking pistons and cylinders of the steam engines rather than attempting to transform them into jet aircraft. Or interstellar spacecraft.

The opportunity to maximize competitive advantage by more effectively leveraging data and data analytics to create the business equivalent of interstellar spacecraft is real, but it requires an insight-driven approach, not a data-driven one. AI-driven data analytics are rapidly evolving; what is novel now will be outdated in two years' time. What we could only dream of doing two years ago is now commonplace. The question becomes, what dreams do you want to be able to realize in the next two years, and what insights would help you achieve them?

Data analytics has the capacity to deliver the insights we need to achieve our dreams. But most data currently live in what I am going to call the 'tool-o-sphere' — a world in which the goal is development of a better dashboard.

I talk a lot about tooling versus transformation. An unfortunate divide has grown between the data world and the executives who are making the key decisions that will shape a business's future. People will point to the hugely significant role that their chief data officer and chief data and digital officer has in their organization, but in my experience, most IT departments see their job as providing tech and tools for the businesses they serve.

There is a worrying disconnect between the people who understand the technology and those who are running the business side. People in the tech sphere come to believe that their job is to provide tools that the organization can use. They provide a catalogue of services that the business might want to consume. People on the business side don't understand the full potential of the technology and continue to pursue what are essentially process management solutions, when the technology has the potential to transform the business — but only if it's asked to deliver insights that have the potential to deliver real, hugely valuable business transformation.

I spoke to a fellow consultant, Lucy (not her real name), about her experience of the relationship between data departments and the rest of the organization. Lucy has a heavyweight background in data science.

The first pandemic lockdown in the UK had been lifted, and I was spending some time in the office, but more time at home. Delightful as it would have been to meet up in the city for a glass of wine, we settled for a virtual meeting.

Lucy and I share a conviction about the transformative potential for the intelligent use of data analytics in business. Sadly, we also share a growing pessimism about the effective use of data in most organizations.

"We've both put a lot of effort into advising industry to use data science capabilities to create new models that have the potential to be, like, nirvana for business insight," Lucy said. "And the way in which these people are orientated is normally in quite small teams. You won't have a team of 100 data scientists in an organization, as you know. Very, very rarely. You might have two or three, or you might have five or six, or 10 or 12. And there'll be a head of data science with whatever is the latest title, you know, CDO or whatever. And what we have seen typically is that the organization is really excited about that. They're delighted they have data scientists because now that means they can solve world hunger and all those other things."

I burst out laughing and nearly choked on my tea. Lucy glanced at me to check I was still breathing and carried on.

"And all you have to do is ask them for some stuff, and they'll do it, and everything will be exciting and wonderful," Lucy said. "And what will happen is two things. One, the business will come along — I've probably overused this, but it's the Henry Ford thing. You know, 'If I'd have asked people what they wanted before I built the Model T, they would have asked for faster horses.' So what happens is that people turn up at the door of the data department and ask for better dashboards. They don't ask for data science. They'll turn up with what they've got at the moment, which is some terrible piece of Excel, or some awful PowerPoint pastiche of a dashboard, and they'll say, 'I want this, but I want it to be updated constantly. I want it living.'

"So what they'll do is they'll basically assemble all the datasets, they'll stick a data visualization tool in front of it and you'll end up with a new dashboard. And okay, you can drill down into it, and you can filter it and make it change when you apply a filter. But it's descriptive, it's diagnostic. There are no algorithms in there, or nothing very interesting. It's just saying, 'Show me the latest sales data.' And if I choose the month, it changes, and the data that feeds it will automatically show me that month, which means I don't need to use Excel anymore and I'm happy! So that's the first thing they ask for — stuff that isn't data science."

There was a brief interruption while Lucy was distracted by something happening in the room. "It's our son George," she told me. "We're having to do the home-schooling thing because the schools are still shut." She disappeared from view, and I could hear some complex negotiations taking place between her and George, involving cartons of juice and something he could do on his tablet for the next half-hour. Lucy reappeared.

"Sorry about that."

"We're doing the same thing," I said. "Only our boy is a bit older."

"Where was I?" she asked, rubbing her forehead a little distractedly.

"Oh yes," Lucy said, her eyes coming back into focus. "The second thing is that everyone will ask for their own version of the same thing. And so what will happen is the head of data, in order to be seen to be performing effectively, will need to serve all of those business functions. So HR, finance, sales, production, they'll all be asking questions, and he or she needs to do stuff for all of them. Go into any organization, and that's exactly what you see — you'll see a data function which is largely just capturing stuff that exists in other line of business systems, putting them into somewhere, be that Amazon or Azure or Google, sticking a dashboard in front of it and doing that for 20 functions. And so what they're really doing is delivering fantastic alternatives to Excel. And the thing is, if you ask the head of the data how she's doing and whether she's serving her business, she says, 'Oh absolutely, everyone's really happy. I'm busy as hell; I need more people. I've got loads of demand, and I'm serving all my business.' And if you ask her boss, he'll say she's doing great work, and everyone's happy with what she's doing, right? But what value is she adding? None. All she's doing is replacing spreadsheets."

Lucy and I chatted about the need for businesses to work more closely with data, essentially to ask more difficult, more valuable questions.

"It does get me depressed at times, "Lucy admitted. "There is so much potential in analytics. We're still only scratching the surface. And I sometimes think, well, why can't the CDO push the company to give analytics some more interesting challenges? But data functions tend to be a bit cut off from the rest of the organization, for the reasons I just described. They're tied up delivering the services the business says it wants, or has been persuaded it wants, and they aren't thinking about the things that could actually transform the business. We're using data analytics to help run the business smoothly. This is your point about how we're still just focused on trying to run things more efficiently; we're not focused on transforming the business.

"There's another thing I've noticed recently," she said suddenly. "It's about industrialization. Scaling things out. Data guys tend not to think about the mode of use of data. Can it or should it be deployed on a tablet, or a phone, or a watch, for example? A lot of data is being used for relatively simple, one-off use, to inform one decision. It's like the equivalent of policy decisions for government. You know, if there's an outbreak of foot and mouth disease, the minister has to decide whether to close farms or not. So the minister gets a whole lot of data presented to them, but the decision is a one-off, black or white. Close the farms or not. But compare that with, say, Uber's peak-time pricing system, which is industrialized — it's live and interactive and it's rolled out to everyone through the app on his or her phone. And I think the lack of real industrialization is a bit driven by the mindset of analysts, you know?"

She glanced at me inquiringly. I made encouraging noises.

"Data scientists are nearly always young," said Lucy. "Typically, very linked to kind of agile ways of working. So they have a backlog of work. They'll do some stuff but they won't do all of it, because they've time-boxed it, and it's a sprint. They didn't do it all, but it was good enough. And they demonstrate that if data science was used, it could predict the price of eggs next Tuesday. And so they think, 'Success, we've done it! We've proved we can predict the price of eggs next Tuesday. Excellent!'

"However, what we need to *industrialize* that information is for it to be accessible by 3,000 people across the business. They need a really easy-to-use application on their phone. Now, the data that feeds the price of eggs application needs to come from 14 systems and that all needs to be automated. The quality of that data needs some real-time data manipulation and quality uplift.

And by the way, we need to push a value back into the core system here, because we're missing that key attribute that we've had to synthesize here to show that we can prove it only if that attribute exists."

I smiled encouragingly again, though, truth be told, Lucy was losing me a bit on the detail at this stage.

"And at that point," she went on, "they'll go, 'Oh, we can't do that. Because to do that you need to have proper data engineering capability, you need to have an IT function that's set up to support these things. You need to have jobs and automation that runs on a regular basis that pulls stuff from systems that we have no approval to use. And actually, we've got to go to the 14 systems to ask to pull data from them on a nightly basis, and two of them have said no, because it will impact their quality of service. Then we need to build some applications that are mobile-ready, and we don't do that in this organization because we haven't got that digital engineering capability.'

"And as a result, it never happens. And what you end up with is everybody going 'Jeez, man, I never knew it was going to be so difficult to industrialize it.' So, all they've really done is tell you that the price of eggs on Tuesday was 37 pence. And when it gets to Tuesday, they can say, 'Look, I was right, the price of eggs is 37 pence.' But you need to place that in the hands of 3,000 egg buyers globally, and you need to do that in real time, so that they can make that decision when the egg market opens at 3 am.

"And that's the point at which they end up with this decision paralysis. They never go beyond the so-called proof of concept. Lots of great ideas and transformational opportunities are left on the cutting room floor.

Because what happens is they then move on to the next one, because the data scientist's job is done. He's created the model. He can predict the price of eggs on Tuesday. He can point at the code — there it is in GitHub. And he's told you the schema for the data that is needed and all of the transforms that he's done. 'My work here is done! And I'm on to the next one because I love doing this fast innovation and finding cool answers to stuff, and now I'm going to predict the price of carrots!'"

I was laughing again. Lucy pressed on.

"And he'll go away and what will happen is that in three months' time, you'll end up with algorithms to predict the price of every vegetable on the planet. But nobody will ever know that, because they never got industrialized. It's the industrialization that drives the value. And part of the industrialization is, how do you roll such a thing out? Is the business ready to adopt it? What are they currently using to price eggs? How do you get them to move from the old egg pricing system to the new egg pricing system? And how do you get them all to consistently use it?

"So, how do you get beyond the data science? How do you get to the value? The data science bit, arguably, is easy, if you've got bright people who know what they're doing, who can work with a business and can work with those data owners who can give access to the data and help them to understand what it is. And you can connect them to the business users who say, 'Here's my problem, here are the characteristics of my problem.' And then they can hopefully say, 'Here's what the answer to that problem looks like.' That's actually the easy bit.

The hard bit is, now make it really usable, automatic, fully supported and available to 3,000 people, reliably, every day."

It was time for Lucy to get back to testing the concept of work-life balance to destruction by juggling her work with George's home schooling. We said our goodbyes and I got to thinking.

Her point about dashboards was a perfect illustration of the tool-o-sphere. Even when organizations have large amounts of data on hand, they often use them for what are essentially mundane purposes. Can I run this process more efficiently? Is there a pattern in product sales that I can use for marketing? If I email customers, on what day of the week do I get the best response? This is like owning a Lamborghini and only using it to do the school run and take stuff to the recycling centre.

Lucy's point about industrialization was also spot on. Data analytics can often deliver a brilliant solution that won't have any practical effect on the business unless it's industrialized, and industrialization is hard. But it isn't just the difficulties of industrialization that can stop insight from becoming useful. Sometimes there are simple organizational reasons — what you might call political reasons — why organizations lack the will or the organizational functionality to be able to extract the real value that an insight has to offer.

A good example of this is leakage in domestic water supply systems. It's an obvious and well-known problem because it gets a lot of attention when water is in short supply — when there's a drought, for example. And whenever water companies say they need to increase their prices, consumers can quite rightly ask why they haven't yet fixed their leakage issues. In times of drought, of course, water companies ask consumers to stop watering their gardens or washing their cars and hosing down their driveways, and to only to flush their loos when they have to. And consumers think, "But if you just fixed all the leaks in your system, we wouldn't have to do this."

Water delivery networks can lose as much as 30% of their throughput through leakage. The UK average is currently around 20%. Which means, even when there is no drought, water companies are having to extract and treat 20% more water than is actually needed, and use up 20% more energy and chemicals in the treatment process. The solution to date has been the obvious one, which is to gradually replace aging, leaking pipes with brand spanking new pipes, which is a slow, laborious, very capital-intensive process. While that process is going on, water companies spend a great deal of time and money fixing the leaks that constantly occur in their aging system.

I'd been involved in a project focused on using data analytics in the field of procurement, optimization and pricing for a chain of retail pharmacies in the US. We were looking at demand prediction and got to the point where we were able to predict that if a certain brand of shampoo was in a shop down the road, rather than the store where it currently was, they were much more likely to sell it. We were predicting demand by store based on local demographics and demand patterns, using machine learning, and were able to optimize the supply chain very successfully based on predictive analysis.

I started to think about how this might be used in utilities, which was a field I was working on at the time, and the obvious approach would be to use the same techniques to predict supply of utilities like power and water. This approach is actually used in the electricity supply industry, where they do some rather sophisticated predictive work to calculate likely demand at any particular time. Some of this is clever, but not actually all that sophisticated, like predicting that millions of people will put the kettle on for a cup of tea after a particularly exciting episode of a popular TV series reaches its cliff-hanging conclusion. The predications ensure that the grid is able to cope with expected, temporary surges in demand.

It's different with water supply because the water network has to be physically full all of the time. If you temporarily reduce the amount of water in the whole system, then a house on a hill somewhere will end up high and dry. Or, if there is a sudden surge in demand, lots of people won't have any water.

I thought about whether we could use predictive analysis techniques to tell us where we were losing water through leaks. If the prediction was that a certain amount of demand exists in any part of the system at any time, and there was more demand than predicted, that might be because there was a leak somewhere.

This is essentially the current technique for detecting leaks. Water companies use data on water pressure and flow collected by a network of sensors in the distribution system to conduct what is called 'night flow analysis' (NFA). Demand for water during the night is very low, and unexpected changes in pressure and flow during those off hours might indicate the presence of a leak. But it is impossible to locate the possible leak with any precision because the District Metering Area (DMA) being measured might be as big as 50 square miles.

The vast majority of leaks are not enormous gushing fountains appearing above ground. We don't see most leakage until it becomes catastrophic, at which time it has been leaking for several weeks, and several hundred million gallons have been lost. Some leaks never become visible, because the water finds some underground route out, like a storm drain.

Even when a leak is known to exist, most techniques used for finding its location in the network of pipes are remarkably unsophisticated. The most common tool is the listening stick, a long, thin steel rod with a sensitive microphone that picks up sounds coming from the pipes underground. The more primitive, but still common, version is simply a piece of stick with piece of hollowed-out wood on the end to fit over the user's ear. Place the end of the stick on a water pipe and the earpiece to your ear, and you can hear the hiss of a leak. The hiss gets louder the closer the operator is to the leak. It's an incredibly low-tech solution, which then leads at best to people digging holes in roads and fields on a relatively speculative basis. They're still likely to dig their first exploratory holes some distance away from the actual leak.

What we needed was another source of data that we might be able to combine with the night flow analysis to provide more information, allowing us to pinpoint leaks more accurately. It turned out that such a data source might exist. Water companies have many years of records of engineers reporting that that they dug a hole outside a house at 27 Station Road, and uncovered a plastic six-inch pipe some four feet down in clay soil, and it had a four-inch radial split that was probably caused by substrate movement. It was a historical record with no obvious value other than as a record of work done, and perhaps to get an analysis of what are the most common types of leaks were, and in what kind of pipe and substrate.

But we found that if we linked that historical data asset to the pressure and flow data from historical NFA reports, we could use machine learning to find patterns in the data. If we looked at the previous night's NFA report, we could identify what was probably a leak, and what was probably not a leak, and provide a far more accurate prediction of the scale and location of the problem, based on analysis of the flow patterns that had resulted from previous, known leaks. The net effect was to potentially reduce the average time between a leak first being detected and it being located and fixed from an average of 28 days to around 12–14 days. It was a transformational change.

We implemented this system for a water company in the Far East, but I have also been talking to water utilities around the globe about how to gain new and immensely valuable insights about leakage from data analysis, but with mixed results.

I don't want to argue that this is the perfect solution to every water company's leakage problem, as there are many reasons why an organization chooses to embrace a new technology or not. But, it's worth highlighting the barriers I encountered in this connection, because they're perfect examples of why insight-led, data-enabled transformational programs are often not taken up or are embraced half-heartedly—in which case they deliver half-hearted results, and everyone congratulates themselves that, as expected, it was never really going to work.

The first thing to say about the water leakage problem is that fixing it or improving it does have the capacity to be genuinely transformational for the water industry. Initiatives that cross silos — linking customer benefits to back-office automation via supply and distribution improvements, for example — can be the most impactful. Changes within silos can be good, but only rarely do they prove to be truly transformational. We look at organizations as a series of linked optimization opportunities. I; if we can introduce a change that affects all or at least most potential optimization opportunities, we can really see results start to happen.

Leakage, for water companies, is exactly such an issue. It affects everything they do: customer supply; customer satisfaction; ongoing production costs; water quality; working capital (because unforeseen leaks lead to additional unplanned work, and regulators have the power to impose huge fines on companies that fail to meet their customer satisfaction targets.) All that, of course, has an impact on the revenue these utility companies earn.

But the real-life obstacles to implementing such a radical transformation are very instructive.

First, and perhaps most obviously, the people with direct responsibility for leakage are not the organization's most senior executives. Offering a 'solution' that radically affects working practices — possibly influencing the way that people have to work in the future, and perhaps reducing the number of people employed, can always face understandable resistance. There can also be issues with unionization. At the grass roots level of any organization, radical solutions are not always welcomed. There can be real resistance to technological solutions that could disrupt industrial legacies.

If, conversely, we look at the people who are most directly in charge of water organizations, there can be other issues. Water companies work to five-year asset management plans (AMPs) that dictate allowable price increases across the period and frame the timeline for meeting customer service and water quality targets. Once five-year programmes have started, with big numbers attached to them, it's not easy for senior management to change tack. The best route is probably long-term, positioning the new data analytics programme as an agent of transformation linked to strategic gains. That's quite a big sell.

Third, implementation of radical data analytics programmes can easily fail. We began work on one programme with a water company, and their IT department took up the challenge. They set out to build the recommended solution, though there is always some 'not invented here' resistance. IT then began to ask senior management for additional funding to build out the tech, without presenting the full, enterprise-wide business case for the benefits it could deliver in financial terms. The programme began to founder.

There was another issue with the implementation: they failed to industrialize the process. They took up the idea and turned it into a tool to input into the existing process, rather than completely reimagining the process, starting with the new insight. In the end, the technology was deployed, but not especially effectively.

We encountered a very similar issue with yet another water company where we built what was meant to be the solution, only to return a few months later to find that they had 'moved on.' Instead of pursuing the prescribed transformation programme, they had used the technology to produce — wait for it — a new dashboard.

I don't mean to be overly critical, because these issues are real, and really difficult, for every organization. But that was an interesting example of how a new data analysis solution with transformative potential can fail to gain traction, or can be adopted in a half-hearted way that fails to deliver the real value it's capable of achieving. We need to recognize the potentially transformative power of data and advanced data analytics. It's time to leave the tool-o-sphere.

9

MOVING BEYOND THE FAMILIAR

One of the obvious problems with the old 'data up' philosophy is that it drives businesses to focus on the data they have acquired and wonder what value they can drive from it. I've spent a surprising amount of time telling clients something I've said several times in these pages: that their data has no value until it is turned into insight. Like oil, it's essentially worthless until it has been refined.

The data that organizations own can be immensely valuable, but they can only tell us about what we have already experienced. They can only tell us about the customers we already have, for example.

One of the joys and challenges of the brave new world of big data is that there is now an astonishing amount of data available about the outside world: from search analysis; from the way people browse websites; from natural language processing analysis of social media, news and commentary, revealing consumers' current interests and concerns. These data take us to a world far beyond the old, imprecise, partial, clunky, after-the-fact information we previously culled from consumer surveys and focus groups. The challenge is to decide how we want to interrogate this ocean of data. What questions do we want to ask? What new insights might have the potential to transform our businesses?

I spoke to Nicky de Simone, The Estée Lauder Companies Inc (ELC) UK & Ireland's Vice President of Enterprise Marketing, Data and ELC Studios. Nicky led a highly innovative insight-led programme that the company implemented in the UK and Ireland. The programme had some precise and challenging objectives, at the heart of which was the idea of identifying 'the unknown customer.'

The proposal was to use a wide range of data sources and advanced machine learning methodologies to identify new customer segments that could not be found through traditional consumer research, and the aim was to build new communities of potential consumers with shared affinities. It was essential that these new audiences could be easily translated into 'buyable' audiences: real people who could be reached via Google search and the key social media platforms: Facebook, Snapchat, TikTok, etc. The ultimate goal was to create rich, creative content and messaging that would engage with these hitherto unknown consumers and take them on a highly personalized journey via their online engagement with the brand – what the marketing gurus describe as an 'omnichannel' approach.

The programme pulled together data from ELC's own customer engagement platforms and outside platforms that use machine intelligence to scan billions of online searches to identify trends in consumer behaviour. It also used insight provided by the company's major retail partners. To this was added web traffic data, social media data, search data and data acquired from market intelligence companies such as Nielsen, Mintel and Experian. These were truly rich data seams. The total amount of available raw data was, quite literally, astronomical.

I spoke with Nicky one grey spring day on a video call. (Whatever happened to people actually meeting other people face-to-face? But never mind.)

Nicky is Italian and comes from the Sorrento region — the northern coast of the Sorrento Peninsula, which juts out onto the Bay of Naples. She speaks perfect English, with just the slightest Italian accent.

"We have been, as a company, very much on a journey," said Nicky. I was instantly transported to an imaginary beach bar just outside Sorrento, gazing across the Bay of Naples. Mount Vesuvius was clearly visible across the bay in the bright sunshine. It was a lot nicer than my office in the City of London.

"We just last week launched within the company a new programme called the Beauty of Data," Nicky told me. "Basically, the whole idea of the Beauty of Data is that we were founded by the most amazing, spirited entrepreneur, Mrs Estée Lauder, over 70 years ago."

The original Estée Lauder was born Josephine Esther Mentzer in 1908. She grew up in New York City, the daughter of a Hungarian mother and a Czech father. Her mother's brother, a chemist, had joined the family in New York and set up a laboratory in the stables of the family home where, among other potentially useful household products, he created a range of beauty creams. The young Esther became fascinated, helping to sell her uncle's products to friends and acquaintances and experimenting with her own recipes. She married her husband, Joseph Lauder, in 1930. They were to have two sons. "I cooked for my family and during every possible spare moment cooked up little pots of creams for faces," Lauder wrote. She memorably said of her quest to find the perfect moisturiser: "Time is not on your side, but I am."

Lauder sold her products in beauty salons in and around New York. There was an important break-through in 1947, when the prestigious Saks Fifth Avenue department store agreed to give her products counter space. Lauder applied creams to customers' skin herself to demonstrate their effect, gave away free samples, offered free 'makeovers' and trained the store's staff in her remarkably effective hands-on sales technique.

In 1953, Lauder launched a product called Youth-Dew as a bath oil that could also be worn as a scent. Youth-Dew empowered women to purchase scents for themselves, at a time when it was customary to receive perfume as a relatively expensive gift. The product encouraged women to wear fragrance every day and not only on special occasions. According to her obituary in *The New York Times* (Lauder died in 2004 at the age of 95), Youth-Dew took her weekly sales at the time from "no more than $400 per week to around $5,000." With impressive foresight into the way the beauty market would develop, Lauder launched the male grooming product line Aramis in 1963 and the allergy-tested Clinique products in 1968. When her company went public in 1995, the initial public offering valued it at $5 billion.[50, 51]

I have a great fondness for legacy companies where the founder's personal influence can still be felt in the organization's culture, so I understood Nicky's very real excitement when she told me her boss was Estée's granddaughter.

Nicky was smiling happily. I smiled too. It was very pleasant to have had the chance to come to this delightful beach bar and talk about business. I imagined myself sipping an Aperol Spritz which, as you know, is a mix of prosecco, soda water and bitters. It was originally invented in Venice in the 1920s. I could imagine Ernest Hemingway enjoying a glass in Harry's Bar in Venice. Or possibly two glasses. It's one of those drinks that tastes perfect in the Italian sunshine but never seems to work its magic back in England. Today, I was enjoying it immensely. Nicky was having a coffee.

"So, the conversations we're having are very much focused on that angle," she continued. "Making every day better for our consumers. In Estée's time, of course, there was no such thing as data. She built a business based on great instincts. And as a company and a portfolio of beautiful brands that have been around for a long time, we have had to make a shift of using great instincts and blending that with great insights.

"What we talk about is really evolution. It's very much softened by the word evolution, but I think those of us sitting a lot closer to it know it's quite a transformation — the ability to use data insights and analytics. A couple of years ago, we scoped out what we called our Enterprise Data Transformation, which was about taking steps along this maturity curve of moving from great instincts into amazing insights, and how we turn those insights into actions."

Nicky told me how the company had spent the previous two years assembling the data into one place, centralizing the team that would be working on it and thinking through how to present information in ways people could understand and turn into action. The initial focus was on delivering meaningful 'intelligence' — the intelligence quotient (IQ) — but it occurred to them that information on consumer behaviour was, in theory, also available to their competitors, and that what would give ELC a competitive advantage was an understanding of consumers' emotional drivers - the emotional quotient (EQ).

"So, the IQ without the EQ or the EQ without IQ doesn't give us the ability to really compete in a way that differentiates us for our consumers," she told me. "When you combine intelligence and emotional drivers — what Jane Lauder, our EVP of enterprise marketing and chief data officer calls 'the math and magic' — you really unlock some beautiful experiences and stories for our consumers. What we said is, we know that we're using similar data, going after similar consumers with products that we believe are much stronger and more powerful, but we need to convince our consumer of that. So how do we get those convincing and compelling stories in front of the right people to really help them make those purchase decisions? We believe that if we use data in the right ways, there are infinite possibilities to reach consumers that are truly 'net new' for our portfolio.

"When you have the new data, the new insights, the more relevant stuff, the more granular, the better your targeting goes," Nicky said. "So, that one pound of marketing spend that may have reached two people previously now reaches four people."

The analysis also allowed them to create far richer, more detailed creative content.

"We were able to tell the creative team that we were about to launch this moisturiser and we needed six different variations of copy treatment, because this person that's looking for the moisturizer is also looking for those men's grooming products, but they're also looking for things that talk about hydration, for example. We were able to build a much more robust brief around what the creative was going to look like in the storytelling, so that we when we show up in social media, show up in search, show up on YouTube, the campaign itself and the story it's telling is far more relevant, based on the new insights that we have."

We chatted about insight-led data analytics, and Nicky came up with a phrase that really resonated with me. "The game changer comes in," she said, "when you *connect* the data, not just collect it. And for us the *connection* of the data, the seeing the insight over here and pulling that data in from over there and analysing this from over here — when you connect all of those things, you have a story, you have an idea, you have an opportunity, you have a challenge that you can start to solve. But when you're just collecting it, you've got a lot of data. And a lot of people at a more senior level making decisions don't understand this data in its purest form, obviously; why should they? So unless it's not just collected, but *connected* for them, it's very hard for them to do anything differently."

⁂

Nicky is a member of an important network of data analysts called ORBIT (Outcome Realized by Insight Transformation). The group is made up entirely of women, which is unusual in the data world, and I am proud to be a sponsor of the network via my work.

I asked Nicky about the group.

"I love ORBIT," she told me. "And honestly, it's one of the most valuable networks that I have been a part of in a very long time, because I think there's not a lot of people that see the world the way we do. I think there's a lot of people that when change is in front of you — change of the size that we're discussing today — it can be very intimidating. And so instead of facing into it, I think human nature is to find ways around it. And the way that shows up in behaviours is you have people questioning data. But although there's maybe numbers that are wrong, if it's directionally right, that still gives us enough of a springboard to go after that change. There's a mindset change that I think has been under-estimated through companies throwing around the concept of big data, and 'data is the new oil,' without really understanding some of the fundamentals.

"I think there's a big change that we've gone through as a society," she concluded, "and it shows up in different behaviours, and it requires different things of people. And I think that can be scary and intimidating. But the ORBIT network brings together like-minded individuals who are driving that change in parts of UK government or in businesses, where historically they haven't been the most embracing of those big, monumental shifts. And it happens that it's all women driving that change in our group. It can sometimes be lonely when you're the change-maker, when you're the one driving all the change, and making everyone uncomfortable and questioning things that they thought they knew to be true for so long. To have that network of very smart, like-minded, strong women in that position has been one of the most rewarding and impactful things I've been a part of in a long time."

I dragged myself away from the bar on the Sorrento Peninsula. The sky outside my office was still grey, and the light on a February afternoon in London was beginning to fade. My Aperol Spritz had magically transformed itself back into a glass of now lukewarm water.

But it had been a great pleasure to talk with someone who shares my belief in the fifth phase: insight-led, data-enabled business transformation.

It's not about *collecting* the data, it's all about how you *connect* it.

10

NEW DRUGS FROM KNOWN ONES: THE BIOVISTA STORY

Aris Persidis and his bother Andreas are the cofounders of Biovista Inc, a privately held biotech company launched in Charlottesville, Virginia in 1996. The company specializes in using big data and a new form of AI called machine building to position known pharmaceutical drugs as broadly as possible, discovering unexpected new uses. The outcomes can be truly transformative, discovering 'nonobvious' drug-disease associations that can lead to significant new applications for existing molecules. This is not only great for patients, who don't have to wait 10–15 years on average for a new medicine, but it also resets the clock on the commercial life of molecules, making it easier and cheaper for pharmaceutical companies to invest more. Biovista's technology is also key to discovering drugs with the potential to treat rare and so-called 'orphan' diseases—those where the small number of sufferers makes research into the disease difficult, or impossible, and the development of new drugs that may treat the condition commercially unviable.

Aris, Biovista's president, has been named one of the World's Top-50 Futurists. His brother, Andreas, the company's CEO, has been named one of the top 100 Leaders in AI drug discovery and advanced healthcare.

* * *

Aris and I first met when we were studying at the University of Cambridge. What brought us together was a shared love of dance; we were both members of the university's Dance Society. He and I and our respective dance partners competed regularly on the open circuit. We were friends then, and we still are, decades later.

I spoke to Aris about the ideas that underpin this book back in November 2020, when the UK was entering its second phase of lockdown during the COVID-19 pandemic. The weather at home in Hampshire was cold and dark. Every once in a while there would be a refreshing downpour of sleety rain. My own general disposition at the time was less than sunny.

Aris and I had arranged to talk via Zoom. When he first appeared on my screen, he seemed to be sitting in a small fishing village somewhere in the Mediterranean. The sun was beating down. Brightly coloured boats bobbed gently in the harbour. The cafés and bars that lined the harbour front were busy serving customers at tables set out on the streets and pavements.

"Tell me you're not really sitting in that place with a glass of wine in front of you," I demanded. Aris confessed that it was a virtual background, and that he was sitting in his Virginia office, southwest of Washington, DC. "But it is a real place," he assured me. "It's the Greek island of Poros. Not Paros; everyone thinks of Paros. Poros is close to the mainland — just off the Peloponnese. We go there a lot."

It didn't cheer me up. "Let's go there now," I suggested. "I could be on the plane in a couple of hours. You could buy me a beer when you get in from the States. Oh, but I forgot! I can't jump on a plane because we're in lockdown." I said this with some bitterness. Aris looked sympathetic.

I smiled grimly. A sudden squall threw heavy drops of wintry rain against the skylight of my study, like a handful of gravel.

"It's nice here today in Charlottesville," said Aris, helpfully. "Sunny and about 66 degrees."

"What's that in Celsius?" I asked, moodily.

"About 19 degrees."

It was clearly time to stop the pleasantries and get down to business. "Right," I said. "Tell me about Biovista. Assume I know nothing, because I'm genuinely not up to speed. Tell me the whole story."

"With pleasure," said Aris.

I sat back and picked up my coffee. The rain on my dormer window had eased to a steady torrent.

"Back in the late '80s," Aris began, "Andrea — my brother — was studying for his doctorate in AI at Strathclyde, after getting his degree in Naval Architecture at Glasgow. I was studying biochemistry at the time, as you know. And I was getting obsessed with a very simple question. Was it feasible to map all drugs — known drugs, approved drugs, drugs in development, drugs that have failed — against every disease and every combination of clinical outcomes?

"And so, the two of us started by compiling a list of drugs, and then we started compiling a list of conditions. And it ended up that there are approximately 273,000 different clinical outcomes that the human condition suffers from. And it turns out that, depending on who you ask and how you count them, there are between two million and 50 million chemicals in the public domain that have some kind of known pharmacology, meaning they're either drugs on the market, or once upon a time they were drugs, or they could never be drugs but are used to investigate drugs, and so on. And we wondered if it was possible to create this enormous map of every drug versus every clinical outcome versus every molecular target.

"But then we had to think, why is this drug connected to this clinical outcome? Well, because of the genes involved, or the specific chemical changes, or the cell types or the organs in the body, or …

"It ended up being 48 or 50 dimensions that we needed to analyse, and then build a map that was constantly changing and constantly evolving. And so we started with this question, and there was no answer to it back in the late '80s, early '90s."

I nodded and smiled, sipped my coffee and settled deeper into my chair.

"Andreas was using AI to design more efficient propeller blades and the keels of ships and boats, and other engineering marvels," Aris continued. "It turned out that computational fluid dynamics require a lot of information, and oftentimes the data is incomplete. So, there's tons of information: incomplete information; incongruent information; contradictory information. And yet, it was possible to design ships and propellers that were very efficient; they actually did a great job. So, tons of information, incomplete information, incongruent information, contradictory information. Does that remind you of anything?"

I felt as if my professor at Cambridge had just cold-called me in a PhD seminar. I put down my coffee and tried to look intelligent.

"Um …"

"It's called medicine!" he said, beaming.

I began to see what he was driving at.

"And then we thought, how about if you take the solutions that seem to work in engineering, and you test them out in this other field of knowledge, which is called medicine? And that was the start. So we used AI solutions originally developed in engineering to start to investigate whether we could answer this monumental question of whether we could create a 48- or 50-dimensional map of the way various molecules might interact with the human body. We were not the only ones asking that question, we were not the only ones trying to answer it, but that was our path."

Aris went on to talk about the astonishing complexity of the human body.

"Every cell in the body is an actor, along with every organelle in that cell. Every protein inside each cell is an actor, and every gene inside every cell's chromosomes is an actor. When you start to think about the number of actors in the human body, it quickly becomes mind-boggling. With trillions of actors all interacting with each other in different ways, the level of complexity is simply staggering. I'm constantly amazed that any drugs work as well as they do. The combinations of possibilities in medicine far exceed the number of atoms in the universe. It's just one of those crazy, crazy things. So, we needed a different doctrine of AI. Not machine learning, because machine learning would simply not work as we know it now. And that's why, in our company, we developed a thing called machine *building*, which is very different."

I was hooked.

Lego and machine learning may seem like an unlikely duo, but for Aris, it was the perfect analogy to describe what he calls 'machine building,' as opposed to machine learning.

"I have an 11-year-old boy and he loves to play with Lego," he told me.

I nodded and smiled. Our son does too. Who doesn't love Lego?

"And he was the inspiration for this analogy because I struggled with finding the right way to describe it," Aris continued. "So he plays with Lego all the time, and at the end of the day the hope is that he will gather up his pieces and put them in a bucket. And let's assume that he does that, which of course he doesn't.

"But if I have my machine learning look at the buckets of Lego each evening, let's say I have 100 buckets. When I show it the next one, it will say, well, because your bucket looks like the 99 that I've seen before, it's likely to have so many Lego pieces in it. And this is how many colours and how many shapes I expect to have in the bucket, because I've been trained on a similar area. But if my little boy puts his shoe in the bucket, which he often does, or puts in a beautiful pebble that he found outside, which he often does, the AI throws a fit and stops analysing. Because it's never seen a shoe or a pebble before. I have to retrain it. So, that's a limitation of machine learning.

And that's where the notion of machine building comes into play.

"What if that Lego piece — that red brick — was everything you knew about one gene? What if that other Lego piece was everything you knew about another gene, and that other Lego piece was everything you knew about a particular chemistry, and so on and so forth? Just like Lego, you can now start to assemble scenarios. This gene plus this gene minus this gene, in this cell line for this disease, but not for that ... what does it look like?"

Aris and Andreas categorized all the bits of information that seemed most relevant to healthcare into just over 100 categories — 103, to be precise, and still counting as of this writing. Next, imagine a Lego piece with 103 studs. A stud about a gene might contain information about other genes that are associated with that gene. Another stud is all about diseases. A stud for a protein would contain information about all of the other proteins that particular protein interacts with in the human body. And so on.

"So, an individual brick represents everything you know with the data you have about an individual thing in medicine," Aris explained. "So far, there are 103 different things in medicine that we feel we need to know: categories like genes, diseases, side effects, drugs, cell lines, animal models, and so on. And in each of these, there is data, sometimes lots, sometimes little. And Biovista have assembled about 10 million of these unique bricks, each with 103 studs. And our machine building takes these individual units of knowledge — these building bricks — and builds scenarios that have never been seen before, and then validates them to see which may work and which may not. It will rank each scenario based on core criteria, to tell you how plausible it may be. And then it will serve to you whatever evidence exists in support or against, and it will compile that ranking for you.

"So, just like with Lego, I will build a bridge by taking 10 Lego pieces and assembling them, and if my assembly is not right, the bridge will not hold any weight. It will collapse, and then I will assemble them in a different way. But it's the same pieces. It's the ability to synthesise knowledge versus the ability to count knowledge. A scenario that today looks implausible may tomorrow be the right one. And so, this idea of false positives or false negatives does not apply to this doctrine of understanding knowledge and risk-benefit analysis. And that's what we mean by machine building."

We talked more about the whole concept of risk and benefit. Aris said that many AI systems in healthcare were trained to assess either benefit or risk, but not both. More fundamentally, he argued that good old-fashioned machine learning is based on historical interpretation. You take what happened in the past, reduce it to datasets and a set of rules, and train a program to match any new data against the existing data.

Which brings us back to machine learning and Lego. What happens when you put a shoe or a pebble in the Lego box?

"Machine learning doesn't actually delve into the *unknown unknowns*," said Aris. "COVID-19 was an unknown unknown. Machine learning two years ago was saying we don't have to worry about SARS-CoV-2 because its genetic sequence is so similar to the flu. It couldn't imagine, if I can put it like that, that a new flu-like virus would have very different consequences for human health.

"It comes back to that complexity I talked about earlier. In typical data analysis, you either have lots of actors but few moves per actor, or few actors and lots of moves per actor. And that's why you can have AI machine learning that can beat you at chess, or it can beat you at Go, or can read MRIs very well, or can navigate your vehicle. Because when you're navigating your vehicle, you actually have very few moves. You move the vehicle front, back, left, right, faster or slower. Your moves are very limited, but you have a ton of stuff around you. Or, in chess, you have two sets of 16 pieces and you have a lot of moves. In an MRI, you have an infinite number of images, but very few ways that these images are different.

"But medicine has got lots of actors and lots of moves. It's like ..."

Aris paused, looking for the right metaphor.

"It's like a wheel has certain properties locked in," he said finally. "I can't improve on the wheel. It's designed in a certain way to do certain things. But as we know, to go on really rocky terrain, say on parts of Mars, a traditional wheel-axle is the most useless thing that you could ever have. It's unfair to ask the wheel to solve that problem. And that's why you have these new crawlers that have the multiple legs, kinds of appendages, and so on. So you basically need the right tool for the job. Now, another way that I think about it is that to a hammer, everything is a nail. And that's very useful if it is a hammer-nail type of problem. But if it's an unknown unknown, what tool do I need to use?

"Machine building moves away from the historical perspective of what happened in the past, and is what's happening now like that or not? And it moves away from the problem of wheels on Mars or hammers and nails.

And it builds entirely new scenarios and basically says, well if 'this,' then maybe 'that.' And it gives us, potentially, a whole new set of insights and new ideas."

In 2011, Biovista launched its Clinical Outcomes Search Space (COSS) platform, which mapped the relationships between drugs and clinical outcomes. This became the basis for the company's drug discovery and repositioning efforts.

In 2020, when COVID-19 had already touched tens of millions of people worldwide, Biovista identified two existing prescription drugs with the potential to alleviate significant symptoms of the disease by slowing down the virus's rate of reproduction to reduce viral load and helping prevent the severe inflammation caused by the disease, which can lead to organ damage. One of the drugs also helped prevent the formation of micro clots in patients' lungs and hearts, another potentially serious consequence of the disease. The repositioned drugs didn't offer a cure for COVID, but they had the potential to improve many outcomes and even save lives.

One particularly unexpected consequence of COVID-19 turned out to be a possible increase in the risk of developing Alzheimer's disease. New research has suggested that individuals with the disease have a considerably higher probability of being newly diagnosed with Alzheimer's within 360 days of their initial COVID diagnosis. "We think of Alzheimer's as something that takes decades to develop," Aris said, "but here it happened in less than a year. And so, you don't have to be a rocket scientist to realize there is a new question to be asked, which is how on God's green Earth did this bug cause this disease?

"And for one of the very few times, it's once in a generation in medicine, we can actually point with a high degree of confidence to specific triggers of the disease. Usually, we never know what triggers a disease. What is it that triggers asthma? Well, we think it's a whole bunch of allergens, but we're not really sure. It turns out that COVID-19 can also bring about epileptic seizures. What is it that triggers epilepsy? The only thing we know for sure is if you're hit in the head and you have what's called a focal injury, that can lead to seizures. For every other case, we have no idea. Maybe there's some genetics, and if there's some genetics, we have no idea what those really mean. But now we see that epilepsy can be an aftereffect of having COVID-19, which raises a question you would never have asked before: how can a virus trigger epilepsy?

"For the first time, now, we know that if you get a specific bug, perhaps COVID-19, perhaps something else, you just upped your risk of these diseases. There are new data coming up all the time, and these technologies can allow us to look at the data in such a way that we can arrive at insights that we never had before."

The machine building techniques devised by the Persidis brothers and their extraordinary team in Athens, Greece (which is where the actual AI tech was developed) are not limited to handling information about drugs, genes and chemistry. The same techniques can be used to explore demographic information about patients, healthcare practitioners (HCPs) and treatment regimes to suggest other unexpected connections. Biovista was consulted as part of the search for a solution to the opioid crisis that's raging in the US, with almost 70,000 deaths recorded as a result of opioid overdose in 2020 alone, and 932,000 total deaths from drug overdose recorded since 1999, the overwhelming majority of which were opi-oid-related.[52] The company analysed prescription data and made the entirely unexpected discovery that the most significant predictor of opioid prescribing patterns was not any particular socioeconomic profile of patients, but the professional education level of the prescriber. HCPs with higher levels of professional education were less likely to prescribe opioids, while doctors with less professional education were more likely to do so. Sub-sequently, new programs were put in place to provide relevant education and training for prescribers, to help ensure that they were making informed decisions about opioid prescriptions.

This AI-driven technology also has the capacity to enable huge leaps forward in what is known as 'person-alized medicine.' This involves treatments that take into account an individual's genetic makeup, medical history and current circumstances. Working with Quantum-Si, a Connecticut-based protein sequencing company, Biovista developed technology to deliver real-life inter-pretations of the outputs of DNA sequencing, giving patients and HCPs accessible information about the health implications of each patient's unique DNA. Com-bined with information from next-generation (but also just-around-the-corner) 'multi-analyte analysers,' which will be able to detect perhaps several thousand poten-tially relevant chemical substances in a drop of blood or saliva, or a nasal swab, this new technology could point to the home-based digital healthcare of the future.

It's what Aris calls 'a doctor on your windowsill,' able to provide instant alerts of health concerns or emergencies and guide patients to any deeper diagnostic or hospital attention they may need.

"The future is perhaps not entirely 'individual', but it is 'individualized.' Medicine will no longer be so broad brushstroke. It will be, 'Who are you? What conditions do you have? What do your genes predispose you to? What is going to work best for you as an individual?'"

I noticed that Aris, on a few occasions, had used the term 'augmented intelligence' rather than 'artificial intelligence' to describe the fundamentals of Biovista's technology.

He argues that there are relatively few instances of the use of AI where no human input is required. The exceptions are essentially when there is a relatively straightforward decision to be made, such as, "Does this visual image match the millions of other images I have been trained on?" Which boils down to a variant of, "Does this set of data match all those other sets of data?"

The use of AI enables us to process exponentially more information that humans are capable of analysing, to detect underlying patterns and suggest possible new connections between what seem like disparate pieces of information. But in every nonstraightforward case, human beings need to evaluate that new insight and decide what its useful application might be. "We are not talking about replacing humans," said Aris, "except in the relatively few small instances which can be mechanized and therefore don't need human input, such as 'that is the same face.' In every other instance, you are basically *augmenting* human intelligence. And that synergy between the human and the machines then becomes incredibly powerful."

One final thought from Aris, which echoes my own thinking. All of the astonishing new insight in the world won't actually change anything unless people have the commitment, the organizational structure and the determination to make change happen.

Thinking about the world of healthcare, Aris says this: "What we have to change, not only in ourselves but also in our pharma partners, is that it's not that you press a button and you get the perfect answer. You press a button, you get the *guidance*, and then your human teams get engaged, and they have been enabled to be much more efficient and effective as a result of the new guidance. And now you are able to make decisions that it would normally take you years to make, on much faster timescale.

"But, are you able and willing to do that? It's not about the technology anymore. It's not what it can generate. It's the politics of decision-making. We are stimulating our industry partners in two directions: one, the power of the insight, and two, the time pressure.

"Because, if you want to be successful with these things, you have to decide to act much sooner.

"Are you able to do that?"

11

LEADING TRANSFOR- MATIONAL CHANGE

The rapid development of what we loosely call AI — machine learning, computer vision, natural language processing and the like — will change all our lives, possibly dramatically. The ChatGPT text-generating chatbot we talked about earlier was released in November 2022. It was based on large language models, which are trained on huge textual datasets of many trillions of words, using machine learning techniques to train itself to offer human-like answers to any question, drawing on something rapidly approaching the sum total of human knowledge.

The debate is already raging over whether this means 'the end of' a variety of important things: the student essay, journalism, legal services, trustworthy news. AI pioneer Geoffrey Hinton, whom we encountered in an earlier chapter as one of the leading figures in the development of artificial neural networks and machine learning, resigned in May 2023 from his part-time role in AI research for Google. Though his resignation seems to have been unconnected to his growing fears about the potential misuse of AI, he said that having left Google allowed him to speak out about his concerns.

"It is hard to see how you can prevent the bad actors from using it for bad things," Hinton told *The New York Times*. "I console myself with the normal excuse: If I hadn't done it, somebody else would." The paper described Hinton as 'The Godfather of AI' and summarized his and others' fears in this way: "[G]nawing at many industry insiders is a fear that they are releasing something dangerous into the wild. Generative AI can already be a tool for misinformation. Soon, it could be a risk to jobs. Somewhere down the line, tech's biggest worriers say, it could be a risk to humanity."[53]

As I said earlier in this book, it is easy to get drawn into debating the various doomsday scenarios that could result from this amazing new technology. My best guess is that we will learn to live with the technology and harness it for good, though there will be people who deliberately use it for bad ends, and there are likely to be occasional unintended consequences of actions that were intended for the good.

Call me an optimist, but I am also a businessman. Whatever uses AI might be put to in the future, it is here, now, and it has the power to transform the way we use data and to create insights that have the ability to transform our businesses.

There is a gravitational pull towards the third phase of business transformation: the use of advanced technologies and hard science to improve our businesses to the nth degree: the 3.4 per million defects of Six Sigma. Advanced data analytics have the capacity to deliver transformational insights, but if — and only if — business leaders have the ability to frame the questions that have the capacity to deliver big, value-creating insights and, equally importantly, the will to lead organizations through the radical change that the insights may require of our businesses. It is relatively easy to improve an existing process by X%, as with the third phase of business transformation. It is exceedingly hard to change the whole way a business operates. Change is difficult. This is essentially a *leadership* problem.

There are two key aspects to this leadership problem. The first is that we are talking about leading organizations in the search for insights that are capable of delivering significant value to the organization as a whole. There has been a very real tendency for leaders to see this as an IT problem; a data problem. It isn't. It's a business problem. I know from experience that a large number of CDOs are now fully integrated members of the leadership team, able to bring their perspective and their expertise to the overall direction of the organization. But, as we have seen, there is still a tendency for senior executives to see 'data' or 'IT' as a provider of clever tools (ever-more-sophisticated dashboards) rather than to involve the departments in the search for radical new business solutions.

The other key aspect of this leadership problem is 'the innovation problem,' and the tendency of all organizations — especially larger, more established ones — to resist real innovation. They are averse to what has been described as 'radical innovation.' I'll address this in a moment.

First, let's go back to the core issue of insight-led, data-enabled transformation. If we are genuinely hoping to transform our organization, it is unfair to ask data departments to come up with the solutions. Any transformation needs to be business-led. The starting point must always be, "What are we trying to achieve? What things, if we could radically improve or change them, could add extra value to the organization — ideally, massive extra value?"

It's not unthinkable that a CDO or a sharp-eyed analyst might come up with such a question, any more that it is unthinkable that anyone anywhere in the organization might come up with such a question. But that's not reasonable and it's not sensible. The leadership of an organization should be best positioned to ask the searching questions that have the capacity to shape the organization's future.

If leaders want data analytics to provide answers to that question, they also need to be able to phrase it in a way that can be dealt with analytically. Whether or not there is a set of data that might be found that has the potential to deliver a solution to the problem is the data analysts' problem. Business leaders don't need to become experts in datasets, but there does have to be a theoretical set of data that could provide the answer. So, for example, "How do I improve my overall profitability?" is too broad a question. There is no possible data-enabled solution that could answer that. But, "How do I identify people who are behaving in ways that are similar to my existing customers, but have not yet been identified by us as potential customers?" (the Estée Lauder 'unknown customer' project that we talked about earlier) is a precise question with a possible data-enabled solution. Biovista's "Can I map every known drug against every disease and every combination of clinical outcomes?" is another.

Business leaders need to work with their data colleagues to explore business ideas that may be capable of a data-enabled solution. I personally believe that there are a vast number of possible data-enabled solutions out there, because there is now a genuinely vast amount of data available to us.

The person who was involved in the UK National Situation Centre, whom I referenced in the first chapter, described going through an identical process with government ministers.

"We put a huge amount of effort into training the analysts who were going to be running SitCen on how to coach the people commissioning the centre to provide answers — basically, government minsters, security chiefs and so on — on how to ask questions," the manager told me. "So that if they asked a question that was a bit rubbish and they couldn't answer it analytically, how were they going to go back to the commissioner — the minister — and kind of say, let's just explore exactly what this question is, so that you're getting the best possible answer."

It was explained to me that that 'a bit rubbish' was typical data-analyst-speak for "there are no data or algorithms in the world that are going to answer that question for you, minister."

"It really is a collaborative process," my contact went on. "The analyst needs to understand the problem that needs solving, and the commissioner needs to come to understand how to phrase the question in a way that can be addressed through data. It's not that hard — questions generally need to be variants of 'How many, how soon, what measurable impact, what happens if … ?' and so on."

The manager went on to talk about another side to the process of helping commissioners get the best results from the Situation Centre team.

"We needed to remind ministers and others that the team that sit in this analytics kind of capability needs to be allowed to experiment and to work in an agile way. So that they have the ability, and are also empowered, to test things. And if something fails like this, you have to build that into the culture — that you fail fast, scrap it, move on, try something else. Now, in SitCen, that was a huge step forward, because that is not a very government way of thinking. And that took a huge amount of trust. The director of the SitCen really fought for that and we made it very clear, from day one, that that was the capability we were building. Fail fast, and the psychological safety to be allowed to work in an agile way and be allowed to experiment. That was built into the DNA of the team."

The second half of the leadership problem centred on our attitude towards innovation. I have written and talked extensively about the concept of innovation. In a book referenced earlier — *My Steam Engine Is Broken* — Jonathan Gifford and I wrote about 'The Innovation Committee,' arguing that all organizations become risk-averse. Even when they recognize that innovation is essential, they want to *manage* the process of innovation, so that it becomes less scary. The only problem with this approach is that it really doesn't work.

We talked about the concept of radical innovation, which was put forward by Wolfgang Grulke in his 2002 book coauthored with Gus Silber, *Lessons in Radical Innovation*.

Grulke distinguishes between evolutionary, disruptive and radical innovation.

Evolutionary innovation is what most established organizations are comfortable with. It looks for constant but gradual improvements in the way an organization operates. This is essentially another version of scientific management and the first three phases of business transformation: experimenting to see how things can be made a little bit better each day.

Disruptive innovation comes in two forms: technological disruption or disruption to what Grulke calls 'market linkages.' A good example of technological disruption would be the way the new cell phone technology disrupted the business model of companies supplying telephone service via landlines. An example of disrupting market linkages would be the effect of the internet on the travel business: airlines, hotels and car rental services suddenly had a whole new route to market, often cutting out various middlemen, such as travel agencies. Radical innovation disrupts everything — technologies and markets. The internet itself is a prime example. Amazon and Uber are others.

It is very difficult for business leaders to put their organization through a process of radical innovation. It requires them to imagine something new and better that has the capacity to destroy their existing business.

The key point is that if we, as leaders, don't keep reimagining our businesses in this way, other people will do it for us. Crazy entrepreneurs with a few million in venture capital have everything to gain and little to lose.

I ran an interesting exercise with the board of directors of a large manufacturing business, with plants in several countries. Many of their product lines were struggling, largely due to competition in the Asian and

Indian markets, but they also had a poor track record of introducing new products, especially genuinely innovative offerings. We had an interesting discussion around how a competitor might go about destroying their company.

I split the board into two halves, and asked one group to think of things they could do to keep the company growing and surviving. The other half were charged with coming up with competitive businesses that were capable of destroying the company. Those who were given the task of destroying their company came up with three times more ideas than their colleagues who were asked to enhance what they did.

We need to engage in a process of 'creative disruption' for our own organizations, because the world is full of people who are trying to disrupt us. If we don't succeed in finding radical new ways to innovate, others will, and leave us in their dust.

Insight-led, data-enabled transformation — the fifth phase of business transformation — is available to business leaders today, and it allows us to safely explore the business changes with the power to radically change our businesses for the better. One of the great benefits of insight-led, data-enabled transformation is that it lets us do a lot of the speculative work in the virtual world.

I spoke with Abigail Brockbank, who was then senior director, data and insight transformation for RS Group, the distributor of industrial and electronics products. We spoke about the company's move towards a more insight-led approach to data analytics.

"If you're thinking about a maturity model and where we are today," Abigail told me, "most companies are using instinct over insight, and what we're exploring is how we move the dial to using insight over instinct." We also talk about it in terms of how we can extend our wisdom, combining our data and insights with our judgement and experience to make better-informed, better-evidenced, unbiased decisions.

"So, how do we become an insight-driven organization, which ultimately is going to get us to extending that wisdom, insight and data? And I think there's a very clear difference, which was, how do you *not* look at it from a data perspective, but how do we look at it from an insight perspective? And I think that was a real light-bulb moment. Because still, in industry, you hear people constantly talk about, 'We want to be data-driven, it's about the data.' But actually, that doesn't mean much, because it doesn't link it back to an outcome, and it doesn't link it back to how are we using insight to drive additional value in the organization."

She talked about the need to involve people throughout the organization, from the most senior executives to the distribution centre floor.

"I think a lot of it is how do you make it feel really tangible. How do you make it relatable, because what we're basically saying is, no matter what role you have in the organization, whether you're in the distribution centre, or in finance, or marketing, you will still be making decisions from data, putting your judgement on top of it, in order to make a decision. And it's about how do we really percolate all of the levels of the organization.

The great news is it's recognized by our senior executive team as a key initiative for us. It's built into our strategy."

Abigail also talked about the need to overlay training and education with practical application, and to bring the programme to life through good communication. In her company, that meant making sure the organization knew about the advances being made and understood the contribution everyone was making to the company's success. She also made a deliberate decision to favour a particular terminology: moving from 'data-led' to 'insight-led,' and from 'data-driven' to 'insight-driven.'

"We've taken this programme from something which three, four years ago was very focused on technology all the way through to something which is actually mainly about mindset, and what else needs to form part of that in order to change your mindset, of which technology and data is one aspect. We talk about how we use data science to be able to better predict where we stock and locate our products. It helps it to feel more tangible for them and gives us a story to talk about it, and then adds into the mindset of 'Look what we've done; look what the art of the possible is.'"

We also talked about something I mentioned earlier, which is the concept of 'value mapping' — seeing the organization as a series of optimization points and identifying those capable of delivering the greatest improvement in value to the organization as a whole, if they are changed or improved.

"One of the things we did was to identify almost like a value catalogue," said Abigail. "So where are those opportunities to drive considerable value, and which of those actually span the whole organization or would support the whole organization? And one of the ones we're picking up at the moment is 'cost to serve.' Do we really understand how profitable we are from a customer perspective or customer group perspective, but also from a product or product family perspective? And that crosses everything. Because I think often when people look at cost to serve, they look at it from more of a silo perspective. So it's, how efficient are we from a distribution centre perspective? That's definitely one part, but we want to take it all the way through the value chain and identify at what point do we get profitability erosion, and what does that mean? How does that affect our operating profit? How does that affect our gross margin? Which is a huge piece of work. But what it will enable us to do as we deep-dive into various parts of it is to challenge conventional wisdom. A lot of it is analysis of the information and connecting the data we've got, but the biggest part then is, how do we make the business change as a result? So again, it goes back to when we're making decisions, and it's evidence-based, but is it unbiased? How do we make sure it's an unbiased decision we're making; that you're not taking on what you think we should be doing versus what the insight is telling us?

"I think the one of the biggest things for us is we are in partnership with the rest of the organization. We're building real partnerships and a collaborative way of working, to go to people and ask, 'What are those business problems you're trying to solve? What are those decisions you're trying to make? And how can we help to support you, to make those better?' We don't talk about data. The language is all about outcomes. It's all about decisions. The data absolutely is critical, but you've got to understand the problems we're trying to solve."

* * *

The fifth phase of business transformation is not going to be about improved quality or efficiency. It is not going to be about who has Six Sigma'd their organization to the point of perfection. The fifth phase is going to be about a bare-knuckle fight to find the most effective business models. Insight-led data analytics have the power to help us discover the most effective business models from the safety of our own offices. We can create virtual models of our core business models and play with them to see which changes produce the highest amount of value. We can view our businesses as a series of optimization points and run the numbers to see which optimizations produce the best results.

The fourth phase of business transformation has been a disappointment. A lot of businesses have drowned in their own data lakes. We have learned a lot about data management, but I can see few real and meaningful business advances that have come about as a direct result. The last decade has been held back by the lingering effects of the 2008 financial crisis. Just when it seemed that economies were emerging from that crisis, they were hit by the effects of the global COVID-19 pandemic and a war in Europe.

There will be continued challenges and further set-backs, but we have a revolutionary new business tool at our disposal in the form of advance data analytics. Many businesses, I think it is fair to say, are still staring at the toolbox, trying to imagine what to do with the complex technologies that lie inside. But there are people who know the answer; they are called data scientists. It is time for business leaders to get together with their data experts and start to reap the benefits of a revolution that is poised to happen: the insight-led, data-enabled transformation of our businesses.

NOTES

1. https://committees.parliament.uk/writtenevidence/37441/pdf/

2. First glimpse inside UK's new White House-style Crisis Situation Centre (telegraph.co.uk)

3. Inside the government's secret data room - BBC News

4. Big data strategies disappoint with 85% failure rate – Digital Journal

5. The End of Theory: The Data Deluge Makes the Scientific Method Obsolete | WIRED

6. Mediterranean diet and life expectancy; beyond olive oil, fruits and vegetables - PMC (nih.gov)

7. Taylor, Frederick W., *The Principles of Scientific Management*, (New York, Harper & Brothers, 1911) Public Domain Kindle edition, Introduction

8. Ibid., p43

9. Nelson, D., "Taylorism and the workers at Bethlehem Steel, 1898-1901," *The Pennsylvania Magazine of History and Biography*, Vol. 101, No. 4 (Oct. 1977) p504 Taylorism and the workers of Bethlehem Steel, 1898-1901 | *Pennsylvania Magazine of History and Biography* (psu.edu)

10. Bedeian, Arthur G., Wren, Daniel A., *Organizational Dynamics*, 2001, Vol. 29, No. 3, pp. 221-225, 2001

11. Taylor (1911), p24

12. Liker, Jeffrey K., *The Toyota Way*, (New York: McGraw Hill, 2021), Second Edition Kindle Edition Location 2684

13. Sapulkas, A., "Young workers Disrupt Key G.M. Plant", *The New York Times*, January 23,1972, p 1. Young Workers Disrupt Key G. M. Plant - *The New York Times* (nytimes.com)

14. Liker, J. K., *The Toyota Way*, Second Edition (New York: McGraw Hill, 2021), Kindle Edition Location 2857

15. UNIVAC and the First Census Bureau Computer: A Brief History | *Time*

16. Smith, W.D., "Getting Along With I.B.M.", *The New York Times*, January 7 1973, p. 1. Getting Along With I. B. M. – The New York Times (nytimes.com)

17. Jacobs, F.R., Weston, F.C., "Enterprise resource planning (ERP)—A brief history," *Journal of Operations Management* 25 (2007), p357-359.

18. The History of ERP | NetSuite

19. Shehab, E.M., Sharp, M.W., Supramaniam, L. and Spedding, T. A., "Enterprise resource planning," *Business Process Management Journal*, Vol.10 No4, 2004, p 364l

20. Shehab et al (2004), p 367

21. Case Study: General Electric (GE) and Lean Six Sigma (6sigma.com)

22. Changing The Corporate DNA (forbes.com)

23. McCarty, T., "Six Sigma at Motorola, *EuropeanCEO*, September- October 2004 Leadership Edition, reprinted with permission: Tower Business Media. Wayback Machine (archive.org) 'Six Sigma Articles.'

24. 01QTEC/33_412 (researchgate.net)

25. Anthony, J., Snee, R., Hoerl, R., "Lean Six Sigma: yesterday, today and tomorrow." *International Journal of Quality & Reliability Management* Vol. 34 No 7, 2017, pp 1073-1093 (PDF) Lean Six Sigma: Yesterday, Today and Tomorrow (researchgate.net)

26. Schroeder, R.G., Linderman, K., Liedtke, C., Choo, A.S. "Six Sigma: Definition and underlying theory." *Journal of Operations Management* 26 (2008), pp536-554. Six Sigma: Definition and underlying theory - ScienceDirect

27. How Six Sigma's history set the stage for its demise (qz.com)

28. Liker, Jeffrey K. *The Toyota Way*, Second Edition. McGraw Hill. Kindle Edition, location 343

29. Ibid., location 858

30. Ibid., location 272

31. Krafcik, John F. Triumph of the lean production system. *Sloan Management Review*; Fall 1988; 30, 1; p 43

32. Antony, J et al (2017) p 1077

33. Codd, E.F., "A Relational Model of Data for Large Shared Data Banks, *Communications of the ACM* Volume 30 Number 6, June 1970, pp 377-387 codd.pdf (upenn.edu)

34. Edgar F. Codd, 79, Dies; Key Theorist of Databases – *The New York Times* (nytimes.com)

35. Tech giants may be huge, but nothing matches big data | Internet | The Guardian

36. Meglena Kuneva - European Consumer Commissioner – Keynote Speech – Roundtable on Online Data Collection, Targeting and Profiling (europa.eu)

37. Data was, Analytics is, the New Oil – *Geospatial World*

38. Big Data PoV_V2.indd (capgemini.com)

39. Connected Futures Cisco Research: IoT Value: Challenges, Breakthroughs, and Best Practices (slideshare.net)

40. Companies Are Failing in Their Efforts to Become Data-Driven (hbr.org)

41. Bostrom, N. *Superintelligence*. Oxford University Press, Oxford, 2014, Kindle edition.

42. Kanaan, Michael, *T-Minus AI*, BenBella Books, Dallas, 2020, Kindle edition, location 2009

43. A Proposal for the Dartmouth Summer Research Project on Artificial Intelligence (archive.org)

44. I.—Computing Machinery and Intelligence | *Mind* | Oxford Academic (oup.com)

45. Kasparov G. *Deep Thought*. Kindle edition, location 1164.

46. Some studies in machine learning using the game of checkers | IBM Journals & Magazine | IEEE Xplore

47. Executive Summary (berkeley.edu)

48. The digitization of the world from edge to core (seagate.com)

49. The man who would teach machines to think – *The Atlantic*

50. Estée Lauder, Pursuer of beauty and cosmetics titan, dies at 97 – *The New York Times* (nytimes.com)

51. Estee Lauder (telegraph.co.uk)

52. Death Rate Maps & Graphs | Drug Overdose | CDC Injury Center

53. 'The Godfather of AI' quits Google and warns of danger ahead – *The New York Times* (nytimes.com)

ACKNOWLEDGEMENTS

I would like to thank everyone who has helped me to develop the thinking that underpins *The Fifth Phase*, which includes colleagues past and present, friends and clients, in particular:

Abigail Brockbank of RS group.

Aris Persidis of Biovista.

Diana Placido of GSK.

Nicole de Simon of Estee Lauder.

Ming Tang of NHS England.

A particular thank you to:

Lee Brown – the best data scientist I have ever worked with – taught me what 'art of the possible' actually meant.

Mark Deighton – has an amazing ability to take complex ideas and concepts and make them clear and easy to understand – taught me how to structure and communicate what was in my head but could never properly articulate.

Andy Fuller – the best data guru you could ever hope to work with – taught me the power of data ontologies and that RAIN is not just water that falls from the sky.

Jen Lowe – her passion and commitment to linking the worlds of data and analytics with the practical realities of business transformation always inspired me – taught me that unless you have everyone pulling in the same direction transformation is not possible.

They all shared my passion and vision that the next concept in business transformation would be 'insight-driven and data enabled'.

The final, and a very special, thank you must go to Catriona Campbell from EY. She believed in and supported this project from the beginning. Without her continued support, encouragement, and enthusiasm this book would never have been written. Thank you.